MW00327539

IMAGES
of America

HUNT'S PIER

IMAGES
of America

HUNT'S PIER

Rob Ascough and Al Alven
Foreword by Ralph Grassi
Introduction by Richard W. Munch

ARCADIA
PUBLISHING

Published by Arcadia Publishing
Charleston, South Carolina

Library of Congress Control Number: 2009941812

For all general information, please contact Arcadia Publishing:
Telephone 843-853-2070
Fax 843-853-0044
E-mail sales@arcadiapublishing.com
For customer service and orders:
Toll-Free 1-888-313-2665

Visit us on the Internet at www.arcadiapublishing.com

To Bob Bright Jr., our friend and one of Wildwood's greatest treasures

CONTENTS

FOREWORD

I feel honored to be writing the foreword to this much-anticipated book by Al Alven and Rob Ascough, which celebrates the "Oceanic Wonderland" that was Hunt's Pier. For many Hunt's Pier fanatics, it will finally justify the passion expressed whenever we gather to reminisce about the pier's wondrous custom attractions and some of its colorful employees, now confirmed Boardwalk legends. Bobby Bright of the Wildwood Historical Society often refers to us as a cult, and by definition, I believe we are. As a local kid, born and raised on the island, this incredible playground was, in a sense, my backyard. My favorite days were those so hot that the crowds would retreat to the ocean, leaving the pier all to me. I would disappear into the Pirate Ship Skua for what seemed like hours. I remember how quickly the cool dampness of the caverns would fade as I entered the arid heat of the upper level of the ship, where the smell of warm musty wood hung heavy in the tilted room and the galley. Upon reaching the bouncy rope bridge, I would often turn around and backtrack through the ride. The old man stationed at the exit knew what I was up to but never made a fuss. One of my earliest memories is when the Keystone Kops ride was in its original location at the back of the pier, where the track bordered the edge, giving a view of the waves rolling in below. I smile when I think about the Golden Nugget tonsorial, and how fascinated I was by the odd-looking fellow waiting to have a shave and a haircut, or how I would hold up the line exiting the Whacky Shack to get a good long look at the creepy hands reaching out of the toilet. I recall gazing lovingly from my antique Kops car at the dancing flapper girls. Little did I know then what an impact Hunt's Pier was making in my life, and by proof of this book, the lives of so many others. So, all aboard—and, as the Flyer sign once reminded us, "Hold Your Hats" as we join Al Alven and Rob Ascough for some super-custom fun!

—Ralph Grassi
Funchase.com

ACKNOWLEDGMENTS

First and foremost, we would like to thank our editor at Arcadia Publishing, Erin Rocha, for her guidance and patience throughout the process of putting together this book.

We also thank Richard W. Munch, founder of the American Coaster Enthusiasts and national roller coaster historian, for providing our Introduction, as well as Ralph Grassi of Funchase.com for contributing the Foreword, and for his invaluable help in compiling information and fact-checking.

We are indebted to the staff of the Wildwood Historical Society and George F. Boyer Museum for granting us access to their amazing collection of vintage photographs; especially WHS president Ann Vinci and museum manager Bob Bright Jr., who not only opened the doors for us (literally and figuratively) on many cold winter mornings but enthusiastically shared their extensive knowledge of local history. Curator Bob Scully and board members Al Brannen and Phyllis Bethel also offered much-appreciated counsel and direction.

Any attempt to chronicle the history of Hunt's Pier owes a great deal to the work of the late Merlin W. Paul, who documented the evolution of the park from its inception. The majority of photographs used in this book courtesy of the WHS, though uncredited, were donated from Paul's estate.

We greatly appreciate the kindness, direction, and encouragement of Hunt family members Evelyn Snooks Bailie and Jane McNutt, the granddaughter and grandniece of William C. Hunt, respectively.

The list of those who provided information, photographs, and direction is a long one. Without the collective cooperation of the following, we could not have seen this project through: former Hunt's employees Michael Blaszczyk, Tom Dormer, Skip Ferguson, Thom Fontannaz, Paul Goodman-Glover, Patrick Herron, Jerry Loewe, Nick McGinty, Salvatore Patrone, Vincent Sculli, and Nick Taweel; local photographer and historian Tom Kinnemand; Lindsey Young and Dino Fazio of the Morey Organization; Kirk Hastings, president of the Wildwood Crest Historical Society; Scott Hand, Diane Pooler, and Steve Miller of Marksman Entertainment, Inc., producers of the *Hunt's Legacy* documentary series; Wayne R. Bahur and Brandon M. Seidl, founders of The Bill Tracy Project; Jan Sherman, assistant vice president and creative director of Sally Corporation; Bill and Seph Cherkasky of darkinthepark.com; Kendell Kelton of Six Flags Over Georgia and Angel Aristone of Six Flags Great Adventure; and Jeanne Sieh of Arnold's Park.

Many individuals and families contributed to this project in a variety of ways, including Wayne Achilles, Mike and Brandi Adamo, Edward Berg, Sean Carragher, Mike and Chris Marie Crater, Steven Felder, Erin Leswing, Ruth Manlandro, Martin Melucci, Bob Mock, David Nelson, James Nocito, "Tiki" Chris Pinto, Marc Scarvalli, Tobias Sheffield, Jackie and Jim Slaviero, Kristen Steindl, Frank Szymkowski, and Bret Ulozas.

Finally, we would like to thank our families, particularly our wives, Linette and Angie, and Al's son Lucas for bearing with us through this long but rewarding process. Your support and encouragement was, in many ways, the most essential contribution to this project.

INTRODUCTION

Looking out over the Wildwoods scene, one can't seem to get away from just how spectacular the setting is, from the moment the sun rises over the Atlantic until the lights of a hundred rides fill the night sky during the warm summers when this small resort comes alive. Each year, this two-mile-long boardwalk swells to a million souls looking for a summer experience, a scene that has been played out for centuries all along the Jersey Shore. The one common denominator has been the group of amusement piers that appears to fit so comfortably within the context of this resort.

The pleasure pier concept started in New Jersey at the original ocean jewel, Atlantic City. Ocean Pier, the first pier in the United States to have public attractions on the ocean, opened there in 1882. It didn't take long for the concept to move south to Wildwood-by-the-Sea near the southern tip of the state. Like its namesake to the north, the new Ocean Pier was the first of its type in Cape May County when it opened in 1906. It was quickly populated with small amusements, games, and attractions of the time.

In early 1935, William C. Hunt, using the profits from his theater empire in southern New Jersey and Philadelphia, purchased the Ocean Pier lot. He rebuilt it on the same parcel, just east of the new boardwalk, providing entertainment and attractions to a population just coming out of the Great Depression. Hunt's Ocean Pier opened with an elaborate ceremony on Saturday, June 29, 1935. The centerpiece was a small wooden roller coaster called the Whirlwind, designed by Herbert P. Schmeck of the Philadelphia Toboggan Company of Germantown, Pennsylvania. The ride would give the Wildwood area two wooden coasters, including the 1919 Jack Rabbit, still popular just south of the Hunt property.

Much of the ballyhoo of that era ended on Christmas Day, 1943, when a massive fire killed two men and destroyed most of Hunt's assets. The fire began near the end of the pier, but winds pushed the flames toward the Boardwalk, spreading them to theaters, shops, and other buildings. Hunt wanted to rebuild immediately, but wartime rationing of wood, rubber, and steel made that impossible. With the pier destroyed, Hunt's new Starlight Ballroom filled the gap for many until Hunt's sons helped rebuild the property into a true amusement showcase just three years after the opening of Disneyland.

The new, all-concrete Hunt's Pier opened on May 30, 1957, featuring only four rides. At the front of the pier was the Flyer, a 36-foot-high junior wooden roller coaster from the Philadelphia Toboggan Company, designed by John Allen and built by James Martz. The pier thrived, and three years later, Allen returned to design the unique Golden Nugget, a combination roller coaster and dark ride with a mining theme that wrapped around and through a three-story, cement-parged building. It would be the company's only steel-track roller coaster and is often considered a response to the first tubular steel-tracked coaster, Disneyland's Matterhorn, opened a year earlier in Anaheim, California.

With the extension of the Garden State Parkway into Cape May County after 1950, the population at Wildwood exploded during the summer. For the first time, all of New Jersey, eastern Pennsylvania, and New York City could make its way to the shore in less than three hours. Meanwhile, the development of the Morey family-owned amusement piers quickly followed the initial purchase and installation of a fiberglass slide in 1969. Bill and Will Morey would eventually build an empire on the Boardwalk with the acquisition of Marine Pier in 1976 (now Mariner's Landing) and Fun Pier in 1984 (now Adventure Pier). With Hunt's Pier losing popularity, the pier and adjacent properties were sold in 1985. Much to the chagrin of roller coaster enthusiasts everywhere, the new owners demolished the Flyer in February 1989 to make way for the 110-foot-high steel roller coaster, the Kamikaze, the largest ride ever built on the pier. It would last only three seasons.

Hunt's Pier was one of the first East Coast parks to include a roller coaster on a pier—Atlantic City was the first. Beginning around 1905, Southern California had many amusement piers with large roller coasters. The Moreys would bring that West Coast flavor to Wildwood in 1996 with the debut of the Great White roller coaster, presently its most popular attraction. For once, the East Coast had its own grand coaster on the beach, reminiscent of the many early West Coast enterprises.

Back on Hunt's Pier, the final venture came in 1996, when new owners opened Dinosaur Beach, built on the popularity of the film *Jurassic Park*. Even adding dinosaur props to the Golden Nugget, then 35 years old, didn't help. After the 1998 season, most of the rides were removed, except for the idyllic Nugget. In response, the Moreys purchased the pier in 2000 and spent the next several years planning a new life for the only remaining ride left on Hunt's Pier in its original location.

Although recognized as one of the leading preservationists on the island, the Morey Organization would come to the realization that moving the asbestos-ridden structure to another pier just wasn't feasible. While brothers Jack and Will Morey were instrumental in championing the cause, they concluded that a multimillion-dollar investment would be better spent attracting the younger crowds that filled the piers every night—possibly with a new roller coaster.

Beginning in December 2008, the track, machinery, and cars of the Golden Nugget were moved to Knoebels Resort in Elysburg, Pennsylvania. It is expected to reopen in 2011, with new stunts and scenery, as the Black Diamond. The rest of the structure was demolished in early 2009, leaving only the ride storage yard and maintenance shops that service the three active Morey piers.

Presently, a proposed wooden roller coaster, which would begin on Surfside Pier and travel to Hunt's Pier over a bridge, is on the drawing board. Before construction can begin, Morey's will have to address the countless regulations and paperwork required to permit erection of the new ride between two piers. Jack Morey called the process "mind-boggling."

Morey's Piers has been established as the largest seaside amusement center in the Western Hemisphere, containing both the largest collection of rides between any boardwalk and the ocean and the best collection of pleasure piers anywhere in the world. Naturally, one of those piers—the one that will eventually contain a portion of the proposed roller coaster—is the old Hunt's Pier. It may never be what it once was, but in a strange set of circumstances, the famous pier will soon welcome its third wooded roller coaster in less than 80 years, indicating its lasting connection to Wildwood's history as well as its future.

—Richard W. Munch
Founder, American Coaster Enthusiasts
Historian, National Rollercoaster Museum and Archives

Author Rob Ascough (right) enjoys a ride on the Mini Hot Rods with his brother, Mike. (Courtesy of Robert and Kathleen Ascough.)

Author Al Alven (right) and his brother, Dave, stand near the entrance to the Flyer. (Courtesy of Albert and Patricia Alven.)

One

Hunt's Amusement Enterprises

At the turn of the 20th century, the resort communities that comprised what came to be known as the Wildwoods were still in their infancies. Activity near the middle of Five Mile Beach, however, foreshadowed the progress to come. Evidence of the dense, jungle-like terrain that gave the area its name was becoming sparse. Large rectangular lots of sand, ripe for development, were now plentiful—some were already occupied by new hostelries like the grand Hotel Dayton or any number of smaller, wooden rooming houses. These diverse accommodations catered to a growing audience, both the wealthy and day-trippers alike. They came by train, the only accessible mode of mass transportation at the time, for the same reasons millions flock to the Jersey Shore today.

The Boardwalk, a relatively fresh concept, was emerging as a social center for both leisure and recreation-oriented diversions. In 1905, Wildwood's first modern amusement center debuted in the form of the spectacular Ocean Pier, located between Poplar and Juniper Avenues. One year later, perhaps by some whim of fate, Bill Hunt arrived in Wildwood via Camden, New Jersey, where he had found immediate success running a pair of movie theaters. It was as an entrepreneur in the motion picture industry that Hunt would establish his business empire in this new home base. By the early 1920s, his theater holdings spread throughout South Jersey and all the way to Philadelphia. In Wildwood alone, he could boast of six successful film houses, including three on the Boardwalk. A true pioneer, Hunt introduced the talking picture ("talkie") to the area in 1929.

While business understandably waned through the Depression years, Hunt's Theatres, Inc., persevered and emerged in strong financial shape. The same could not be said for the owners of the struggling Ocean Pier. In 1935, the Wildwood Pier and Realty Company sold the pier to Hunt, who had become not only one of the island's most successful businessmen but also a respected civic leader. His determination to improve the pier and transform it into an entertainment showplace would set the stage for the future of the Boardwalk.

W. C. Hunt

William Cecil ("Bill" or "W.C.") Hunt was born on March 13, 1872, in Port Jefferson, New York, the son of William E. Hunt, a shipbuilder by trade, and Sussana E. Bishop. He received his formal education in Bridgeport, Connecticut, before finding employment with the United Illuminating Company at age 17. After that, he spent two years working for the Novelty Advertising Business, gaining valuable experience operating a chain of 28 stores. He married Mabel Disbrow, a native of Mount Vernon, New York, and together the couple had four children—Ruth, William ("Bud"), Guy, and Evelyn. In 1906, Hunt ventured to Camden, where he opened one of the country's first nickelodeons in addition to the 80-seat Bijou Dream Theatre. Later that year, he purchased a $1 excursion train ticket to Wildwood. Instantly enamored with the young resort's untapped potential, he opened his first shore theater at Atlantic and Garfield Avenues. (Courtesy of the Wildwood Historical Society.)

Shortly after settling in Wildwood, Hunt was hired by Gilbert Blaker to manage the famed Blaker Theatre at Atlantic and Cedar Avenues. He would go on to operate the Bijou, Casino, Comique, Crest, and New Avenue Theatres. Over time, Hunt's talents as a master promoter came to the forefront. He eventually acquired the Blaker, around which he would build his own movie theater empire as well. (Courtesy of the Wildwood Historical Society.)

The Strand Theatre at Boardwalk and Maple Avenue was one of 17 movie houses that were part of Hunt's Theatres, Inc., by the early 1920s. This included 10 theaters in Cape May County and seven more in South Jersey and Pennsylvania. Hunt was known for meticulous upkeep of his theaters, some of which were renovated and expanded multiple times to keep up with modern standards. (Courtesy of the Wildwood Historical Society.)

Success in the theater industry made Hunt a household name throughout the region and led to additional business ventures. On the Boardwalk, he built the ornate Hunt's Plaza between Oak and Cedar Avenues. Featuring a large auditorium that held nightly dance contests and appearances by nationally renowned performers of the big band era, this was a major center of activity during the war years. (Courtesy of the Wildwood Historical Society.)

As if the grand marquee wasn't enough, the smaller southern entrance to the auditorium was also designed in elaborate fashion. Hunt spared no expense when it came to both the interior and exterior presentations of his businesses. This included permanent signage as well as temporary advertisements, such as this portrait promoting an appearance by Phil Emerton's Diamonds orchestra. (Courtesy of the Wildwood Historical Society.)

By the late 1940s, renovations had allowed for larger commercial units to be built into the complex's facade. The former Hunt's Plaza—now marketed as Hunt's Starlight Ballroom—lost some of its decorative ambiance but evolved into a more modern, multifunctional entity. It became the epicenter of the emerging dance hall/nightclub scene of the Wildwoods. (Courtesy of the Wildwood Historical Society.)

Facing direct competition from nearby Convention Hall and large dance halls in Atlantic City, Hunt booked top name orchestra leaders like Tex Beneke, Woody Herman, and Charlie Spivak. Soon, the rambunctious sounds of rock 'n' roll "record hops" filled the hall. To Hunt's credit, his operation changed with the times and so continued to thrive. (Courtesy of the Wildwood Historical Society.)

As the years passed, Bill Hunt's list of accomplishments continued to grow. In addition to presiding over his entertainment empire, he served as a state assemblyman and senator, was president of the Wildwood Trust Company, and was a prominent member of the Greater Wildwood Chamber of Commerce. He was also a founding member of the Wildwood Golf & Country Club and was one of the first to campaign for a passenger boat service from the southern tip of New Jersey to Delaware (the eventual Cape May–Lewes Ferry). This publicity photograph was taken in the 1950s, when Hunt owned and published the weekly *Wildwood Leader* newspaper. He is flanked by his sons, Bud (left) and Guy, both of whom served under him as Hunt's Enterprises executives. They would eventually inherit full control of their father's investments. Standing at center is Bud Dry, the Hunts' longtime bookkeeper. (Courtesy of the Wildwood Historical Society.)

Published by R. W. Ryan.
The New Ocean Pier at Wildwood-by-the-Sea, N. J.

Hunt's crowning acquisition would be that of the landmark Ocean Pier in 1935. Seen shortly after its completion in this c. 1905 postcard, Wildwood's first modern amusement center was designed by Philadelphia-based architect Charles A. Brooke and constructed at a cost of approximately $150,000 by the firm of Thomas Goslin and William Brannan. (R.W. Ryan.)

Inspired in design and function by the large pleasure piers in Atlantic City, Ocean Pier's various offerings challenged the existing local competition—most notably Blaker's Pavilion and the Casino Pier—to keep pace. The emergence of these entertainment centers during the early 20th century helped put the Wildwoods, as shown in this c. 1906 postcard, on the map as a vacation alternative to Atlantic City and nearby Cape May. (R.W. Ryan.)

Conformed to accommodate up to 10,000 guests at one time, Ocean Pier's two-story central pavilion initially featured eight bowling alleys, pool tables, shuffleboard and basketball courts, and a grand carousel, in addition to a huge ballroom and a first class vaudevillian theater. Note that the main portion of the Boardwalk (directly in front of pier) and the North Wildwood stretch (which began at Twenty-sixth Avenue) had not yet been positioned to run parallel to each other. When Bill Hunt acquired the lot, he had the large pier reconstructed to the east of the new boardwalk—a massive undertaking deemed necessary as the beach continued to expand. The main north-south drag in the middle of the photograph is modern-day Surf Avenue. While only a smattering of structures—mostly rustic hotels, wooden rooming houses, and small summer cottages—existed on the frontier-like island at the time, dramatic change was coming. A building boom would soon fill in the sandy patches of real estate that lined the unfinished streets of the burgeoning resort. (Courtesy of the Wildwood Historical Society.)

By the mid-1930s, the Wildwood Pier and Realty Company found itself in poor financial shape. Cash-strapped after years of operating the pier at a deficit during the Great Depression, the company found a willing buyer in Bill Hunt. The theater tycoon purchased the property for approximately $200,000 and immediately began to plan improvements. (Courtesy of the Wildwood Historical Society.)

Hunt invested in many new rides and attractions, but a simple addition to the lobby of the pier's Laff Theatre ended up being one of the most memorable. Constructed by the Old King Cole Papier Mache Company of Canton, Ohio, and supplied through the Philadelphia Toboggan Company of Germantown, Pennsylvania, Laffing Sal waved her arms and greeted visitors with an endlessly playing recorded laugh. This version was photographed at the Musee Mecanique at Pier 45 on Fisherman's Wharf in San Francisco. (Courtesy of the Wildwood Historical Society.)

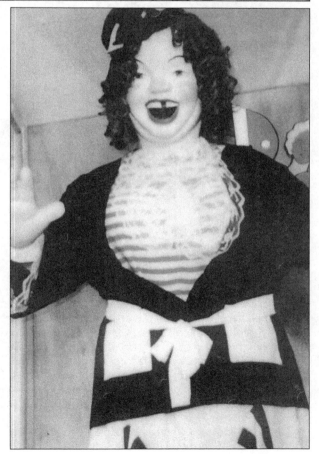

The Ferris Wheel presents to you Wildwood from a birds eye view.

View of net-work that provides For those thrill-a-minute rides.

A large portion of Ocean Pier was dedicated to new rides installed by Bill Hunt to increase the pier's appeal to families. Among the new arrivals advertised in this promotional material was the Ferris wheel from the Eli Bridge Company of Jacksonville, Illinois. Another addition was the Whirlwind roller coaster, designed by legendary coaster creator Herbert P. Schmeck of the Philadelphia Toboggan Company. The success of these attractions, along with a fun house, Whip, and giant Kelly slide, led to the addition of more popular ride concepts in subsequent years. Future seasons would see the debuts of such attractions as the Jack and Jill slide, the Mirror Maze, and the Witches Forest, a haunted walkthrough. The pier advertised 40 attractions at the bargain cost of 40¢ per ticket, a major concession to the budget-conscious patrons of the era. (Ocean Pier promotional material; courtesy of the Wildwood Historical Society.)

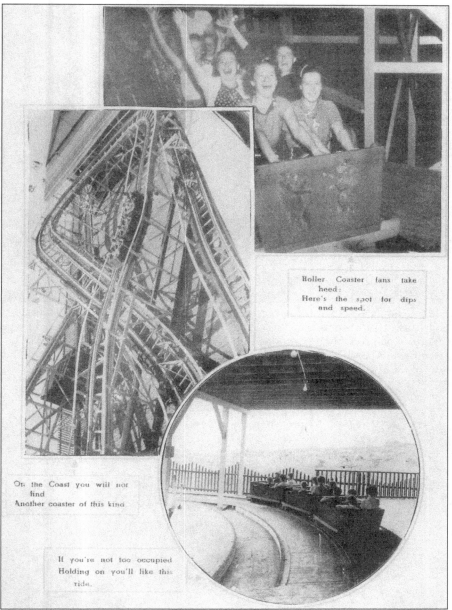

Roller Coaster fans take heed:
Here's the spot for dips and speed.

On the Coast you will not find
Another coaster of this kind

If you're not too occupied
Holding on you'll like this ride.

The Whirlwind was designed specifically with children in mind. The figure-eight layout featured shallow dips and gentle turns instead of the dynamic drops and high-speed curves of other thrill machines of the era, such as Playland's popular Jack Rabbit—a John Miller–designed coaster that had debuted in 1919. Roller coasters similar in nature to the Whirlwind were constructed in amusement parks across the country and still operate at Little Amerricka in Marshall, Wisconsin, and Six Flags Great America in Gurnee, Illinois. Perhaps most significantly, the installation of the Whirlwind marked the first major collaboration between the Hunt family and the Philadelphia Toboggan Company. Some 22 years later, this company would be contracted to build the premier attraction for Hunt's new pier, beginning its important role in the development and evolution of Ocean Pier's successor. (Ocean Pier promotional material; courtesy of the Wildwood Historical Society.)

A second pier would eventually be put on the drawing board after Ocean Pier was destroyed in a spectacular fire on Christmas Day, 1943. A night watchman and Wildwood firefighter perished in the blaze, which took more than one million gallons of water to finally douse. The origin was determined to be accidental, despite speculation of a German U-boat attack off the coast. (Courtesy of the Wildwood Historical Society.)

The most destructive fire in the resort's history claimed not only Ocean Pier but also more than 30 nearby businesses and 12 apartment houses. Among the popular institutions lost were Nixon's Baths, Sagel's Candies, and the Surfside Hotel. With World War II ongoing and the country's attention diverted, the future of the Boardwalk—and the Wildwoods in general—was uncertain. (Courtesy of the Wildwood Historical Society.)

Two

LAYING THE FOUNDATION

The loss of Ocean Pier dealt a severe blow to the Boardwalk and the community at large. Any thoughts Bill Hunt had of rebuilding had been put on indefinite hold due to a lack of resources during and immediately following the war. In the meantime, the always-busy Hunt focused on his other ventures, including the modernization of several of his Wildwood theaters and attracting local orchestras to play at the Starlight Ballroom. Hunt was rejoined in the daily operation of his enterprises by his sons, Bud and Guy. Both had served as amusement and theater managers before they left home to serve their country. Together, they would secure the future of the family business.

By the mid-1950s, when plans for a new pier were being finalized, the Wildwoods were in the midst of a dramatic transformation. Postwar prosperity, the advent of automobile travel, and the completion of the Garden State Parkway had given birth to a new kind of resort. The island was evolving into a paradise for middle-class vacationers, as families flocked to the shore in record numbers. They arrived in glistening Bel Airs, Packards, and Thunderbirds, while hundreds of sparkling new "motor inns" sporting similar names welcomed them with open arms. As was the case when Ocean Pier was conceived a half-century earlier, the Wildwoods were primed for the addition of a contemporary amusement resort. The construction and opening of the new Hunt's Pier in 1957 was met with great fanfare.

Wary of the fate of its predecessor and so many other Wildwoods landmarks, the Hunts wisely opted to build with fireproof materials. The presence of concrete in favor of wooden planks gave the pier a sleek, modern appearance. The premier attraction, the Flyer roller coaster, was an instant and enduring hit. Strategically positioned at the northern side of the pier where it met the Boardwalk, it would go on to beckon generations of riders with the promise of an "over the ocean" flight adventure.

The Flyer was the first of many imagination-capturing custom rides that the Hunts would introduce in the years to come.

A major milestone in the Wildwoods' history is celebrated as (from left to right) Bud Hunt, operations manager Vince Kostek, Wildwood mayor Ralph James, and Guy Hunt open the gates to Hunt's Pier. The new "Talk of the 'Walk" unofficially debuted on Memorial Day, May 30, 1957, with the Flyer roller coaster and three other rides. Starting on June 14, the pier was open nightly. It would take less than one summer for Hunt's Pier to establish itself as the Wildwoods' premier amusement center, despite competition from Marine Pier, Playland, and the Casino Arcade to the south and the subsequent debut of the Ramagosa family's Sportland Pier a few blocks north. The Hunts had instant advantages over their rivals in their abilities to cross-promote with their highly-successful theater operation and advertise throughout the region in the various newspapers owned by Bill Hunt. (Courtesy of Wildwood Historical Society.)

Construction of the new pier began on October 14, 1956, at the former site of Ocean Pier. Aggressively promoted by Hunt's Enterprises as the first all-concrete pier on the East Coast, it was assembled at a cost of approximately $250,000 and would initially cover close to 55,000 square feet. (Courtesy of the Wildwood Historical Society.)

Project superintendent Harry Witte, a former Wildwood fire chief, was credited with conceiving the idea of a concrete pier. The timbers in the water beyond the end of the structure are the charred remains of Ocean Pier. They would be removed one year later to accommodate the new pier's first expansion. (Courtesy of the Wildwood Historical Society.)

Witte (far right, with hat) keeps watch as workers pour green-pigmented concrete to create the pier's deck. While this method was costly and time-consuming compared to the traditional method of building with wood pilings and planks, it was a worthwhile safeguard against fire. Another benefit was that large attractions could be added without the need to rebuild sections of the pier. (Courtesy of the Wildwood Historical Society.)

Vincent J. "Vince" Kostek Jr. was hired to manage the pier prior to its construction. He would serve in the same capacity for the duration of the Hunts' ownership tenure. Kostek was a hands-on operations professional who brought creativity and a youthful exuberance to the job. He and his crew would handcraft many of the pier's most famous attractions. (Courtesy of the Wildwood Historic Society.)

Another familiar face throughout the years was that of Merlin W. "Merle" Paul, the Hunts' publicity workhorse and theaters manager. Always equipped with his camera, Paul captured the essence and evolution of Hunt's Pier from every angle, particularly for use in promotional materials and other advertising campaigns. Much of the existing documentation of Hunt's Pier is due to Paul's tireless work. (Courtesy of the Wildwood Historical Society.)

First employed by Hunt's Theatres in 1937, chief projectionist Harold Sherwood also became directly involved in the operations of the amusement pier. In addition to having joint ownership of several rides, including the Scrambler and, later, the Keystone Kops, he was the troubleshooting coordinator of the pier's sound systems and wrote dialogue for various dark ride stunts. (Courtesy of the Wildwood Historic Society.)

Once construction of the pier's concrete deck was completed, a crew from the Philadelphia Toboggan Company arrived to begin work on the headline attraction for 1957—the Flyer roller coaster. The ride would be the first designed by John C. Allen, a longtime employee who returned to the company to serve as president and chief executive officer after a brief absence. (Courtesy of the Wildwood Historical Society.)

The first part of the Flyer to rise was the curved loading platform, which was a design element common to Philadelphia Toboggan Company roller coasters of the era. As the Flyer was being constructed, identical copies of the ride were being built at Angela Park in Drums, Pennsylvania, and the Gooding Park Zoo in Columbus, Ohio. (Courtesy of the Wildwood Historical Society.)

The Philadelphia Toboggan Company sent James Martz to Wildwood to supervise the erection of the coaster. Martz, a veteran of more than 50 previous coaster projects, is seen here surveying the Flyer's far turnaround as a carpenter works on the wood catwalks that preceded the installation of the layered wood track. (Courtesy of the Wildwood Historical Society.)

An American flag placed atop the Flyer's lift hill celebrated the "topping off" of the highest point of the structure. Once completed, the roller coaster stood 36 feet tall and featured nearly 1,000 feet of track. However, the structure appeared much larger because of its placement and the fact that it towered over the pier's other early attractions. (Courtesy of the Wildwood Historical Society.)

Two trains, each consisting of four cars that held four passengers each, arrived on site and were installed during the later stages of the coaster's construction. The flanged wheels, similar to those used on railroads, were common to Philadelphia Toboggan Company junior coasters, which were smaller, less intimidating versions of the white-knuckle thrillers that made the company famous. (Courtesy of the Wildwood Historical Society.)

As construction of the Flyer raced to completion, other rides were installed on Hunt's Pier. The Turtle, supplied by Traver Engineering Company, was a smaller version of the Tumble Bug rides that were commonly found in amusement parks across the country during the early part of the 20th century. (Courtesy of the Wildwood Historical Society.)

In the spring of 1957, crowds strolling the Boardwalk could see Hunt's Pier in its final stage of preparation. The Flyer was nearing completion, missing only sections of track, handrails, and signage. The coaster's wooden frame had already been painted bright white, allowing it to stand out dramatically against the backdrop of the Atlantic Ocean. (Courtesy of the Wildwood Historical Society.)

One of the final details to be completed was the installation of the Flyer's signage, which featured oversized letters positioned to face southwest. Day or night, when the sign glowed a deep red hue, it was clearly visible as far down as Cedar Avenue—not coincidentally, near the entrances of the rival Casino, Playland, and Marine Pier amusement centers. (Courtesy of the Wildwood Historical Society.)

A ride on the Flyer began with a slow climb to the top of the lift hill, which provided a fantastic view of the Atlantic Ocean as the train crested the peak of the incline. After a short pause, the cars would plunge down the first drop into the heart of the structure. Upon rising again, the train sped around the far turnaround "flying" directly above the surf near the back of the pier. The remainder of the one-minute ride featured a series of gentle drops and curves as the train made its way back to the loading station. In an example of how subtle, seemingly innocuous touches would become such an essential component of the pier's appeal, the hand-painted "HOLD YOUR HATS" warning became one of the Flyer's most enduring taglines. (Courtesy of the Wildwood Historical Society.)

Hunt's Pier was an immediate success, attracting large crowds even during the traditionally slow afternoon hours when most were busy enjoying the sand and surf. The Flyer was particularly popular with children who found the coaster to be thrilling but not overly intimidating. The placement of the ride at the base of the pier proved to be a masterstroke for high-volume business. (Courtesy of the Wildwood Historical Society.)

When the Flyer's train hit the brakes after the final stretch of bunny hops, a sea of laughter and smiling faces was a common sight. Once the train pulled into the loading station and the lap bars were released, the race was on to see who would be first to get back in line for another ride. (Courtesy of the Wildwood Historical Society.)

For riders who found the Flyer to be a little too extreme for their tastes, Hunt's Pier featured a noteworthy collection of kiddie rides, such as these helicopters. The rotating sign in the foreground that advertised the pier as an "Oceanic Wonderland" would go on to become one of its most recognizable icons. (Courtesy of the Wildwood Historical Society.)

A Scrambler from the Eli Bridge Company was part of the inaugural ride lineup. Though a staple at amusement parks today, the Scrambler was a new concept and one of the most sought-after attractions in the industry at the time. Hunt's ability to add such a ride helped set the pier apart from the competition. (Courtesy of the Wildwood Historical Society.)

In addition to the Flyer roller coaster, the Philadelphia Toboggan Company supplied eight Panther Cars and 1,710 feet of track for $8,500. Since real estate on the pier was extremely limited, the ride was installed around and beneath the roller coaster's structure to allow space for other rides to be allocated elsewhere. (Courtesy of the Wildwood Historical Society.)

The layout of the Panther Cars meandered through Blockville as well as various scenes depicting children's nursery rhymes. This was also the first location of "Paul Bunyan," a large fiberglass figure that would eventually make its way to other high-profile locations on Hunt's Pier as it was expanded in future seasons. (Courtesy of the Wildwood Historical Society.)

The perimeter of the Flyer's structure was used for the Pennsylvania Railroad, Ltd. The miniature train was styled to resemble a modern diesel locomotive and featured open cars. Installation included the railroad ties and track being set on a gravel bed carved into the pier's deck. (Courtesy of the Wildwood Historical Society.)

After passing the Flyer's far turnaround over the ocean, the Pennsylvania Railroad traveled the north side of the pier next to the roller coaster. It then curved again, underneath the ramps leading toward the loading station, before coming to a stop. (Courtesy of the Wildwood Historical Society.)

Amusement rides were not the only form of entertainment offered on the pier. The Hunts were often able to use their Hollywood credentials to bring in unique acts including Zippy the Chimp, who portrayed Cheetah in the Tarzan movies. The lovable primate performed three times a day for children during the park's inaugural season. (Courtesy of the Wildwood Historical Society.)

A heavy emphasis was placed on the appearance of pier employees. A clean, professional look with white shirt and black dress pants was mandated. Like Walt Disney, the family wanted to make sure their amusement park had little in common with seedy carnivals that were giving the entertainment medium a bad reputation in the years following World War II. (Courtesy of the Wildwood Historical Society.)

Hunt's Pier enjoyed a successful debut, which made possible new additions for the 1958 season. A Satellite Jet from Kasper Klaus of Germany arrived during the offseason. This was an enhanced version of the company's Roto Jet rides, one of which could be found on nearby Sportland Pier. The ride was the first of its kind in North America. (Courtesy of the Wildwood Historical Society.)

The Satellite Jet allowed riders to pilot their own spacecraft by controlling the height of the cars as they rotated around the center boom that pivoted once the ride got up to full speed. Because of the country's fascination with space travel during the mid-century era, the ride's theme was a big hit. (Courtesy of the Wildwood Historical Society.)

Another new addition for the 1958 season was the Crazy Cups. Supplied by the Philadelphia Toboggan Company, the ride was a smaller version of the company's popular Cuddle Up. The new rides were not only instant favorites, they attracted the attention of other amusement park operators from around the country who came to Wildwood to see the Hunt's operation for themselves. (Courtesy of the Wildwood Historical Society.)

Constructed in 1955 on the west side of the Boardwalk opposite the future home of Hunt's Pier, Ocean Center was a 10-unit commercial complex that was home to various shops and game operators leased by the Hunts. Like the pier that would follow, it was constructed of concrete and steel to safeguard against fire. The 1958 season saw the opening of Skyline Golf on the roof of the building. (Photograph by Tom Kinnemand.)

By placing Skyline Golf on the roof of Ocean Center, Hunt was once again able to maximize space. Real estate on Hunt's Pier that would otherwise have been allocated for the miniature golf course was instead used for future expansion, featuring custom-designed spectacles as well as the latest and greatest off-the-shelf flat rides. (Courtesy of the Wildwood Historical Society.)

Bill Hunt's reputation as a successful businessman and community leader elevated him to local celebrity status. The official dedication of Skyline Golf was attended by, from left to right, North Wildwood mayor Anthony Catanoso, Wildwood mayor Ralph James, Bill Hunt, unidentified, and Wildwood Crest mayor Ed Nesbitt. (Photograph by Tom Kinnemand.)

With the opening of Skyline Golf, Hunt's Pier evolved into an all-inclusive entertainment complex. Ocean Center's indoor concessions were assurance that money was made even when the weather wasn't conducive to outdoor amusements, such as the Shore Plaza, built in 1962 by Will Morey and visible at the lower right. The timing of the complex couldn't have been more appropriate, because in the years that would follow, many of the old-style shore resort hotels that lined the side streets of the island would be replaced with state-of-the-art motel accommodations better equipped to cater to modern families. Many came from affluent suburban areas and were able to take advantage of the nation's ever-growing interstate highway system. Consumer tastes were quickly changing, and Hunt wanted to make sure that he was a step ahead of his competition in the Wildwoods. The goal of adding a theater to the complex would be realized within the next decade. (Photograph by Tom Kinnemand.)

Ever the showman and promoter, Hunt keenly used his various businesses to promote one another. The lobbies of his movie houses were often used to preview future Hunt's Pier attractions. On display here at the Strand Theatre at Boardwalk and Maple Avenue was a Panther Car and a collection of exotic-themed props that would become part of the pier's next major attraction. (Courtesy of the Wildwood Historical Society.)

Jungleland, the headline addition for the 1959 season, was heavily publicized around the region. This advertisement, prominently displayed in a window at the Shore Theatre at Atlantic and Schellenger Avenues, previewed the new ride. The debut of Jungleland signaled the start of a period of rapid expansion that would see Hunt's Pier evolve into one of the East Coast's premier amusement centers. (Courtesy of the Wildwood Historical Society.)

Three

An Oceanic Wonderland

The early success of Hunt's Pier ensured the additions and further investment that the Hunt family had planned all along. Over the next few years, methodical expansion would bring to life many of the pier's most beloved rides and attractions. During this process, the influence of the recently opened Disneyland theme park in Southern California was prevalent. It first manifested in 1959 with the creation of Jungleland, which was no doubt inspired by Disney's iconic Jungle Cruise. Though considerably smaller and less elaborate than its influential West Coast counterpart, the ride was unlike anything else ever seen on the Boardwalk.

Jungleland's debut also marked the beginning of the Hunts' working relationship with prop master Bill Tracy, who designed many of the ride's stunts and scenes. Tracy, a Cape May County resident and emerging force in the amusement industry, would play an important role in the evolution of Hunt's Pier, as most of the major attractions constructed through the next decade would receive his creative touch. This included the Hunts' premier addition for the 1960 season and perhaps its all-time most beloved icon, the Golden Nugget Mine Ride. A hybrid roller coaster and dark ride designed and built by the Philadelphia Toboggan Company, the Nugget whisked riders through abandoned mine shafts filled with spelunkers and the myriad of obstacles that got in their way. The Nugget survived longer than any other of the super-custom rides on the pier, existing through all of the post-Hunt incarnations.

In 1962, the Hunts unveiled the Pirate Ship Skua, a walkthrough attraction inspired in part by fun houses and the Noah's Ark attractions of days gone by. Tracy was once again contracted to install various props, along with the local firm of Messmore & Damon. With features such as a tilted room and rotating barrel, the Skua was a favorite of many and one of the pier's most recognizable landmarks. By the mid-1960s, Hunt's Pier not only reigned as the unquestioned showplace of the Boardwalk but was regarded by many in the industry as the number-one seaside amusement pier in the world.

The signs read:

SEE THE MAD WITCH DOCTOR

SEE THE ELEPHANTS AT THE WATER HOLE

SEE CHARGING CROCS!

SEE WHAT HAPPENS TO THE STRAY MISSIONAIRES

SEE PANARAMIC VIEW OF A FLOWERED JUNGLE

SEE FIGHT TO DEATH BETWEEN NATIVE BOY & CROC!

SEE FAMILY OF FRIENDLY HIPPOS

Taking cues from Disney's famous Imagineers and their own film industry–inspired roots, the Hunts sought not merely to fill their pier with rides—they wanted to create memorable adventures for the entire family. Theming and presentation were key, and no small detail was ignored. Though the Flyer visibly loomed in the background, patrons' eyes were diverted to the decorative ambiance of Jungleland, complete with bamboo poles, thatched tiki huts, and other exotic stylings. Marketed as if it were a real life, interactive movie serial, Jungleland beckoned pier visitors to journey through the mysterious rivers of the African continent as part of a search party to locate a lost missionary and schoolteacher. Simple but effective hand-painted signage helped tell the story of the attraction before a ticket to the ride was handed over. Conceptually, it was not unlike the way movie trailers are sold to the public today. (Courtesy of the Wildwood Historical Society.)

Once a necessary expansion of Hunt's Pier was completed, construction began on the 6,000-square-foot Jungleland, a joint venture created by Allen Hawes, Jamie Sanford, and Bill Tracy. The first parts of the ride that took shape were the tunneled finale built of concrete blocks and the loading platform featuring rough-hewn timbers. (Courtesy of the Wildwood Historical Society.)

While Jungleland was designed to resemble a river, the ride system called for a guide rail mounted to the pier's concrete deck with boats that rolled on tires. A minimal amount of water would be used to disguise the rail and make it seem as if the boat was floating in an actual body of water. (Courtesy of the Wildwood Historical Society.)

Shown above is Bill Tracy, as depicted on the cover of his first full catalog for Outdoor Dimensional Display Company in 1962. Born in Toledo, Ohio, in 1916, Tracy was an art director for Ringling Bros. and Barnum & Bailey Circus in Sarasota, Florida, before starting his own firm. Jungleland was among his earliest amusement park projects. (Courtesy of Wayne R. Bahur and Brandon M. Seidl, billtracyproject.com.)

Jungleland was constructed of relatively simple props and stunts that, when put together, presented a single cohesive scene. The designers' attention to detail created amazing depth for a ride on a small boardwalk amusement pier. Workers spent many hours carefully crafting a fantastic faux tropical landscape that would serve as the attraction's immersive environment. (Courtesy of the Wildwood Historical Society.)

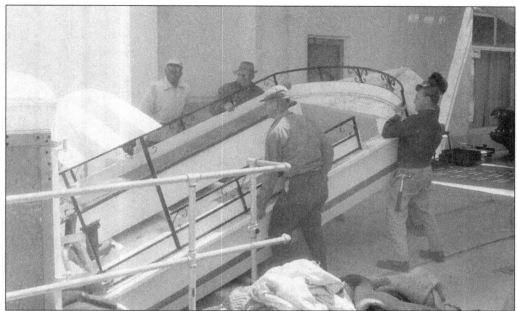

Jungleland's four passenger boats—the *African Queen*, *Congo Kitty*, *Jungle Belle*, and *Swamp Lilly*—held 14 riders each and arrived in shipping containers via railroad. They were pulled through the Ocean Center complex by Vince Kostek (above, right, with hammer) and crew before being brought to the construction site, where they were quickly installed in time for a late-June debut. Each boat was manned by a tour guide and equipped with a dispatch radio and speaker system. Mimicking the interactive nature of Disney's Jungle Cruise, this allowed operators to both outline the rules of the ride and enhance the attraction with colorful, and often humorous, commentary. (Both courtesy of the Wildwood Historical Society.)

Jungleland immediately became the Boardwalk's most-talked-about attraction. By the middle of August, the ride had already carried 100,000 riders, thanks in part to intense promotion throughout the region. Its success led Bill Tracy to find a successful market for similar installations in other parks, such as Hershey Park in Hershey, Pennsylvania, Palisades Park in Fort Lee, New Jersey, and Riverside Park in Agawam, Massachusetts. The Hunt's original, however, remained unique, despite the rides that it inspired throughout the years. A "Jungleland" that later appeared on Fun Pier was clearly Tracy-inspired but was not known to feature any of his actual designs. (Both courtesy of the Wildwood Historical Society.)

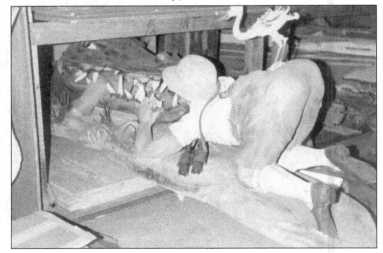

Like the Flyer, Jungleland was squeezed into a tiny patch of real estate on Hunt's Pier. The lack of barriers within the ride's layout made the environment seem expansive, even though the same scenes were visible on more than one occasion throughout the outdoor portion of the ride. (Courtesy of the Wildwood Historical Society.)

In addition to Jungleland, the 1959 season saw the debut of the gas-powered Hot Rods. A precursor to modern-day go karts, the Hot Rods allowed patrons to race Mercedes-Benz replica sports cars on an oval track. The Panther Cars located beneath the Flyer were renamed the Mini Hot Rods to connect the two different rides. (Courtesy of the Wildwood Historical Society.)

Another new addition in 1959 was a Tilt-A-Whirl ride from Sellner Manufacturing. The uniquely shaped cars lent to the ride's name, Tilt-A-Shell. Like the Scrambler that debuted on Hunt's Pier in 1957, the Tilt-A-Whirl was a new concept found in Wildwood before it became commonplace at amusement parks across the country. (Courtesy of the Wildwood Historical Society.)

After just three seasons, Hunt's Pier was on its way to becoming a full-fledged amusement park. The Flyer and Jungleland were already the two most popular rides on the Boardwalk, anchoring a growing roster of attractions that could be enjoyed by families. The Hunts had laid the blueprint for success and would soon follow up with further eastern expansion. (Photograph by Tom Kinnemand.)

In 1960, Hunt's Pier was extended another 160 feet to accommodate the landmark addition of the Golden Nugget Mine Ride. Seen with its wood-and-steel-frame under construction, the attraction was positioned on the south side of the pier, opposite Jungleland. There, its progress could be easily viewed by curious beachgoers and Boardwalk strollers. (Courtesy of the Wildwood Historical Society.)

The Nugget was another product of John Allen and the Philadelphia Toboggan Company (PTC), which combined a roller coaster with a traditional dark ride to create one of the more original amusement park experiences of the time. Under construction in this photograph was the first of two short lift hills that carried the mine cars to the roof of the structure. (Courtesy of the Wildwood Historical Society.)

Unlike the nearby Flyer, the Golden Nugget's track was constructed of steel. Not only was it the first and only steel-tracked roller coaster designed and built by the PTC, it was only the second steel roller coaster in the country. The first, Disneyland's Matterhorn Bobsled by Arrow Development, debuted the previous year. (Courtesy of the Wildwood Historical Society.)

The completed structure featured a rock-like facade that gave the Nugget the appearance of a mountain with mine shaft openings. The northern side, which also housed the loading platform, was decorated with a veneer consisting of Old West–style buildings, including a saloon, bank, and barbershop. (Courtesy of the Wildwood Historical Society.)

Initially, the platform was uncovered and exposed to the elements. Similar to the common sight of smiling faces on the Flyer as the coaster's cars pulled into its station, those returning to the Nugget's point of entry expressed disappointment only that the ride had reached its conclusion. (Courtesy of the Wildwood Historical Society.)

Strict attention to detail was maintained with ride operators given uniforms specific to the Golden Nugget. The ride's theme capitalized on the popularity of television and movie westerns of the day, such as *Bonanza* and *Gunsmoke*. It also continued the adventurous tradition of Jungleland, though from a setting standpoint, the two pier icons could not have been more different. (Courtesy of the Wildwood Historical Society.)

After climbing two lift hills, the runaway mine car traversed the top of the structure. There, riders would encounter cowboys and Indians, a covered wagon, the requisite old prospector, and Boot Hill Graveyard. If one could take their eyes off of the scenery, this vantage point also offered terrific views of the rest of Hunt's Pier, the beach, and the Boardwalk. (Courtesy of the Wildwood Historical Society.)

One of the Nugget's most memorable props was this skeletal cowboy and his horse. Note the detail, with the not-so-recently deceased gripping his arrow-pierced chest. He's also still brandishing his gun, while his trusty steed is eternally undaunted in its attempt to drink from a trough. This ghastly scene sat near the entrance to the ride's dreaded Bottomless Shaft. (Courtesy of the Wildwood Historical Society.)

Much of the indoor portions of the ride were dimly lit or kept in total darkness, creating the feel of an actual mine. The boxed shape of the wooden cars and the powerful smell of the greased tracks and musty interior only added to the experience. After plunging blindly down the Bottomless Shaft—in reality, a short drop that felt much steeper in the dark—riders were whisked into the heart of the structure. There, they encountered several scenes like the one above, depicting two treasure-seekers preparing to dynamite their way into another shaft. All manner of obstacles lay ahead, including a variety of Bill Tracy props such as a giant spider and a charging wolf, along with a rotating tunnel, falling barrel, and waterfall stunts. Because it was technically a roller coaster, the fast-paced nature of the ride enhanced many of the traditional dark ride scenes. (Courtesy of the Wildwood Historical Society.)

On the second level, the mine car made a hairpin turn, briefly appearing outside before disappearing into another shaft. A high-pitched whistle, which could be heard from blocks away, bellowed as the runaway vehicle careened around this stretch of track. In addition to being one of the ride's highlights, this was a clever selling point to pier visitors on the midway below. (Courtesy of the Wildwood Historical Society.)

The Golden Nugget was the largest addition for the 1960 season, but Hunt's Pier also expanded with industry-coveted iron rides. The Jumpin' Jupiter, supplied by the Allan Herschell Company of Tonowanda, New York, was a rampless roundabout similar to the "flying coaster" rides that were becoming popular at the time. (Courtesy of the Wildwood Historical Society.)

Located near the Golden Nugget were the Venetian Swings, which allowed a pair of riders to control the height of their gondolas by pulling on ropes attached to an overhead structure. It was another product of the Allan Herschell Company, a longtime supplier to the amusement industry whose roster of rides were found in parks large and small. (Courtesy of the Wildwood Historical Society.)

The Hunts continued to import flat rides from Europe when the Calypso from Mack Rides arrived in 1961. The spinning ride featured an elaborate lighting display that turned it into a spectacle for both riders and onlookers when the sun went down. It would be the precursor for many similar rides to come in future years. (Courtesy of the Wildwood Historical Society.)

Hunt's Pier was again expanded to make room for another major custom attraction in 1962. Once more, John Allen and the Philadelphia Toboggan Company were contracted; this time, the concept was an elaborate pirate-themed walkthrough fun house. Atop a stationary base, a ship would be constructed. It was then expertly engineered to rock back and forth through the installation of an internal hydraulics system. (Courtesy of the Wildwood Historical Society.)

The frame of what would come to be known as the Skua began to take shape over the winter of 1961–1962. The structure was positioned directly behind the Golden Nugget, at the back end of the pier's south side. Once finished, it often gave off the impressive visual impression that a ship had run aground on the beach. (Courtesy of the Wildwood Historical Society.)

As with Jungleland and the Golden Nugget, Bill Tracy was hired to design various stunts for the new ride. By this point, Tracy was widely regarded as a creative genius who brought his ideas to life through simple engineering. He was joined in the creation of the ride's special effects and scenery by fellow industry leaders George H. Messmore and Joseph Damon. (Courtesy of the Wildwood Historical Society.)

Various props included a maniacal caveman, an enchanting harem, and an assortment of animatronic pirates that accosted patrons. As with other Hunt's Pier attractions, good-natured gags and humor were essential components of the presentation. A talking parrot, beleaguered cook, and a skull ensemble parody of *Sing Along with Mitch* were all part of the fun. (Courtesy of the Wildwood Historical Society.)

Posing on the deck of the ship prior to its maiden voyage are, from left to right, unidentified, Hunt's assistant Al Evans, Bud Hunt, Joe Ranaldi of Palisades Park, Guy Hunt, ride designer Jack Ray, and Bill Tracy. Amusement park officials from all over the country continued to visit Hunt's Pier to inspect new custom rides and attractions. (Courtesy of the Wildwood Historical Society.)

The ship was painted bright shades of blue and orange to give it added visual weight and was outfitted with authentic masts, sails, and various pirate flags. Combined with these carefully-created design elements, the gentle sway of the vessel was an impressive sight from all vantage points. The menacing skull-shaped entrance, visible at lower right, was one of the final details crafted to complete the Hunts' latest masterpiece. (Courtesy of the Wildwood Historical Society.)

The new attraction was featured prominently in this full-page advertisement, which appeared in the 1962 Wildwood Hotel, Guest Home, and Apartment directory. It was officially christened by Wildwood mayor Ralph James and 15-year-old Wayne Achilles, who won a model-building contest and the honor of choosing the name Skua, after a carnivorous Antarctic seabird. Like the custom classics that preceded it, the ride was an instant hit. Riders delighted in exploring the dark caverns and tunnels below the ship and an eventual trip up to the outside deck. The most popular portions of the Skua were the fun house–like challenges within the ship, which included a bouncing drawbridge, maze, mirrored room, and—most fondly remembered of all—the famous tilted room in which the floor was actually slanted. Because it was a walkthrough attraction, the Skua offered the pier's visitors yet another unique amusement experience. (Hunt's Pier promotional material.)

The 1963 season would see the addition of the Devil's Inn. A portable trailer-mounted dark ride from the Allan Herschell Company, the ride was brought to the pier by being passed through the open middle section of Ocean Center. From there, it was pulled across the Boardwalk and to the rear of Hunt's Pier. (Courtesy of the Wildwood Historical Society.)

Though it was a simple, carnival-like installation, the Devil's Inn drew large crowds due to its impressive exterior presentation. The ride's tenure would be very short, at least in this incarnation. The following year, it evolved into what became one of the Boardwalk's most fondly remembered haunts. (Courtesy of the Wildwood Historical Society.)

The Hunts continued to use their celebrity connections to help promote various attractions throughout the 1960s. Movie and television star Mickey Shaunessey was one of the pier's most famous patrons, as seen here getting in touch with his inner child on the Mini Hot Rods. Other visitors of note included Paul Anka, Joey Bishop, and the Lennon Sisters. (Courtesy of the Wildwood Historical Society.)

Wet Boats, also manufactured by the Allan Herschell Company, were a popular addition in the early 1960s. Each boat was capable of carrying four children and featured a bell for enthusiastic clanging in the front and back seats. For many young Hunt's Pier visitors, this and similar kiddie rides served as early amusement experiences. (Courtesy of the Wildwood Historical Society.)

While Hunt's Pier was known to debut new rides and attractions on a yearly basis, older investments were given a new lease on life with simple updates. The Scrambler that debuted for the 1957 season was relocated to make room for new rides and was given an updated theme and name—El Scrambler. (Courtesy of the Wildwood Historical Society.)

Hunt's Pier was quickly becoming known as a showplace for super-custom rides like Jungleland, the Golden Nugget, and the Skua. Still, space was allocated to include a vast collection of flat rides like the Tip Top. Manufactured by Frank Hrubetz & Company, this dynamic installation featured spinning tubs set on an angled turntable that rotated and bounced up and down. (Courtesy of the Wildwood Historical Society.)

Four

PACING THE FIELD

At the start of the 1960s, the amusement industry was in transition. Intimate neighborhood parks, on the decline for two decades, were closing in record numbers as theme parks began opening in metropolitan areas. Theme parks were much larger than traditional parks and boasted amenities such as convenient parking, one-price admission, elaborate entertainment, and state-of-the-art rides in a setting that invited patrons to escape from reality. The future of the industry was filled with uncertainty, yet the advent of the theme park was not the only thing that would shape the evolution of Hunt's Pier.

Competition on the Boardwalk hit a fever pitch in the late 1960s and early 1970s. Ramagosa's Sportland Pier, an amazing showcase for rides imported from Europe, was gaining popularity. A stone's throw north of Hunt's Pier, the Morey family began planting the seeds of their own amusement empire, as Surfside Pier would come to blend the best aspects of traditional amusement parks with incredible theme park–style attractions. Meanwhile, Marine Pier and Fun Pier, despite a lack of standout attractions, provided viable competition to the south. Still, there was little doubt as to which entity ruled as the Boardwalk's 800-pound gorilla through the 1970s. The Hunt family understood that it could never rest on its laurels, and amid competition—locally and from parks in New Jersey, Pennsylvania, and beyond—continued to feature new rides and attractions that catered to guests of all ages.

Several Hunt's Pier rides received new leases on life by evolving into more elaborate attractions. The Devil's Inn, installed in 1963, would be transformed into the Whacky Shack the following year. Similarly, an antique car ride to be known as Keystone Kops was enclosed and renovated prior to the 1967 season. Both attractions would be relocated on the pier in 1970, when real estate was needed for the Hunts' next big attraction. The Log Flume was Hunt's Pier's first direct response to the national theme park trend and was the kind of expensive attraction that separated the modern parks from the older competition.

As Hunt's Pier completed its first decade of operation, it was already established as one of the most noteworthy seaside amusement parks in the world. By the early 1960s, the pier had expanded to nearly twice its original size. As the Wildwoods continued its evolution as a seaside resort, the pier grew right along with it as a super-custom showplace. To the immediate north, directly on the beach, stands Odger's Restaurant and a miniature golf course; by the end of the decade, this would become the site of the Morey family's Surfside Pier. Three blocks north of Hunt's (just out of view here) was Ramagosa's Sportland Pier, which would also grow steadily in the seasons to come. (Above, courtesy of the Wildwood Historical Society; below, photograph by Tom Kinnemand.)

The most notable change for the 1964 season was the addition of the Whacky Shack. In typical Hunt fashion, the ride was previewed with creative signage that inspired curiosity and intrigue with an added sense of humor. Not only did clever advertisements build anticipation for individual attractions, they kept patrons guessing as to what the Hunts would come up with next. (Courtesy of the Wildwood Historical Society.)

The Whacky Shack was a remodel of the Devil's Inn dark ride that had been installed the previous season. The interior and exterior of the portable ride were reworked by Bill Tracy, who replaced the original demonic theme with one that was more moody and mysterious. (Courtesy of the Wildwood Historical Society.)

The exterior of the Whacky Shack featured many of Tracy's visual hallmarks, including slanted towers, crooked windows, and distressed-wood clapboards. The letters that spelled "WHACKY SHACK" rocked from side to side, an eye-catching detail that was designed to grab the attention of passersby along the pier's bustling midway. (Courtesy of the Wildwood Historical Society.)

Tracy thoroughly worked over the interior of the Devil's Inn, adding some of his most popular stunts and scenes, including a forced perspective doorway, a skeletal old woman in a rocking chair spinning spider webs, and devilish creatures preparing a human meal in Hell's Kitchen. A particularly gruesome visual featured a woman being split in half by a gigantic motorized buzz saw. (Courtesy of the Wildwood Historical Society.)

A memorable scene included this eerie clock, complete with a shrieking bird that emerged from the face as soon as riders approached. Tracy believed that the element of surprise was often as important as what riders could easily see. Unlike other collaborative efforts, designing the Whacky Shack allowed Tracy the freedom to more extensively explore his creative boundaries. (Courtesy of the Wildwood Historical Society.)

The 1964 season saw other key additions to the pier. The Pennsylvania Railroad received a new C.P. Huntington train from Chance Rides, built to resemble a traditional steam locomotive. Now named the Iron Horse, a covered station was constructed, and for the first time, the train was placed on the track to run in a clockwise direction. (Courtesy of the Wildwood Historical Society.)

The Iron Horse still took riders around the base of the Flyer's structure. A new addition was Ghost Town Junction, at the far end of the layout. This seemingly abandoned Western outpost was inhabited by skeleton gunfighters. Occasionally, the train stopped here as actors decked in outlaw garb "robbed" the conductor and those on board. (Courtesy of the Wildwood Historical Society.)

Another new arrival was the Himalaya from French company Reverchon. Typical of many of the European flat rides the Hunts imported, it featured a dazzling lighting package that made it almost as much fun to watch as it was to ride. The area around the Himalaya became a popular hangout for teenagers, who bopped and danced to the rock beats emanating from within. (Courtesy of the Wildwood Historical Society.)

The classic carousel is often considered the heart and soul of an amusement park. Most parks featured one, and Hunt's Pier was no exception. Since the pier debuted long after the days of large, ornate machines created by master carvers, a smaller portable piece was purchased from the Allan Herschell Company. The ride, elegant in its own right, was positioned on the north side of the central midway, near the front of the pier. There, it was tucked snuggly amongst many of the more popular attractions, such as the Flyer, Iron Horse Railway, and Jungleland. (Both courtesy of the Wildwood Historical Society.)

The Hunt's Pier entertainment area not only included the amusement pier but also the Ocean Center complex across the Boardwalk, which featured various leased shops, Skyline Golf, and eventually, the Ocean Theatre (opened in 1965). The new movie house was the northernmost of the six Hunt's theaters in Wildwood. It would play first-run films for years to come. Rain or shine, there were many ways for customers to spend their money at a Hunt-owned venture. This was vital, as the summer season was short, and one extended period of foul weather could be damaging to any business. (Both courtesy of the Wildwood Historical Society.)

Debuting with considerably less fanfare than other rides and attractions were the Antique Cars, an electric vehicle ride with a guide rail system manufactured in Germany by the Jhle Company. It featured a simple layout designed to conform to the small area behind Jungleland. (Courtesy of the Wildwood Historical Society.)

The Antique Cars gave children the opportunity to drive replica Ford Model Ts around a winding path on the pier's north side, overlooking the ocean. Along the way, various props and scenery were passed, including a "new car garage," period gas pumps, and this clever nod to the Hunt family's famous movie theaters. (Courtesy of the Wildwood Historical Society.)

For the 1967 season, Hunt's Pier turned an old ride into a new one simply by enclosing a portion of track. The ride was subsequently transformed into Keystone Kops, themed after the Mack Sennett comedy troupe of the 1920s. While it technically became a partial dark ride, its goofball presentation kept the mood light and amusing for children. (Courtesy of the Wildwood Historical Society.)

Keystone Kops featured a short trip through a cartoon world filled with various stationary and animatronic characters created by Jamie Sanford of American Enterprises, Inc. The ride began in an indoor, fluorescent-lit setting before traveling outside behind the rear of the main structure and heading inside again. Along the way, the cars passed through a seemingly endless succession of crash doors. (Courtesy of the Wildwood Historical Society.)

The pier's next headline addition would be the Log Flume in 1970. Designed and constructed by Arrow Development of Mountain View, California, the ride's layout included an elevated rapids section followed by a dramatic splashdown. In the days before water parks, log flumes were a novel concept, as guests could cool down without having to leave the pier. (Courtesy of the Wildwood Historical Society.)

Completed at a cost of approximately $400,000, the Log Flume's trough was supported by tall timber poles which gave the attraction a visual theme that allowed it to blend in with neighboring Jungleland. A Plexiglas screen was installed at the bottom of the splashdown plunge to prevent those on the pier below from getting soaked. It worked—usually. (Courtesy of the Wildwood Historical Society.)

Decked out in their Sunday best, longtime Hunt's fixtures Harold Sherwood (front) and Bud Dry were game to participate in one of the Log Flume's test runs. After snapping this photograph, Merle Paul also joined in the fun, as did the majority of the pier staff. (Photograph by Merle Paul; courtesy Ralph Grassi, Funchase.com.)

The installation of the Log Flume was significant because it gave Hunt's Pier something that other small amusement parks lacked. From the time log flumes started being constructed in the mid-1960s, they had only been featured in the nation's larger theme parks. Hunt's version enabled the pier to compete with theme parks many times its size. (Courtesy of the Wildwood Historical Society.)

The use of forced perspective in the pier's architecture—another tried-and-true Disney trick—made the Log Flume's structure seem much larger than it actually was. From this angle, the ride appeared to tower over Jungleland, but in reality, the apex of the flume was less than 50 feet from the base of the pier. (Courtesy of the Wildwood Historical Society.)

Unlike many of its theme park contemporaries that incorporated multiple plunges, the Log Flume featured a single splashdown. At the time, the Hunt's Pier ride was a state-of-the-art attraction. Like all of the heavily promoted custom rides that came before it, the new headliner attracted large crowds and quickly attained unofficial landmark status. (Courtesy of the Wildwood Historical Society.)

"Paul Bunyan," the familiar lumberjack statue, was a natural fit among the tall timbers and river-bound logs of the Wildwoods' newest attraction. Initially, the oversized fiberglass figure had been situated within the Flyer's layout amid the nursery rhyme characters of Blockville. Later, he was moved to sit atop the wooden fence along the pier's midway that kept the main portion of Jungleland from view. The design of the flume included a large neon sign that spelled out the ride's name on the north side of the structure and a horizontal ledge that would serve as the lumberjack's new perch overlooking the middle of the pier. (Left, courtesy of the Wildwood Historical Society; below, photograph by David Nelson.)

A familiar installation at smaller parks, the Flying Bobs found a home on Hunt's Pier during the 1970s. A product of Mack Rides of Germany, this flat ride featured attractive signage and a Swiss Alps theme. It was yet another version of the high-speed spinning rides made popular at German fairs such as Oktoberfest. (Courtesy of the Wildwood Historical Society.)

For the little ones, an Umbrella Ride from Hampton Rides was added. Unlike some kiddie rides that offered only a single-vehicle riding experience, this one featured a menagerie of cars, trucks, and motorcycles that rotated around a circular platform in a fashion similar to that of a carousel. (Courtesy of the Wildwood Historical Society.)

Keystone Kops was eventually relocated to the south side of the pier, closer to the front entrance. An expanded indoor section was accompanied by an outdoor area that took riders along the beach. Before returning toward the loading area, the cars curved around the Firehouse 5 band figures, which rank among Jamie Sanford's most memorable character creations. (Courtesy of the Wildwood Historical Society.)

Flapper dancers swayed to the beats of the music inside, greeting riders out front on the loading platform. Other characters that inhabited Keystone Kops included clowns, a barbershop quartet, and bumbling police officers. The ride inspired a series of signature creations that went on to represent other attractions, including One-Eyed Jack (Skua), Cactus Pete (Golden Nugget), and Crazy Dan (Jungleland). (Courtesy of the Wildwood Historical Society.)

80

As the Atlantic Ocean receded, Hunt's Pier grew in lockstep with the ever-growing beach. After starting out with a handful of rides in 1957, the pier expanded numerous times to include a well-rounded collection of attractions that rivaled the greatest amusement parks of the time. (Courtesy of the Wildwood Historical Society.)

The Hurricane Slides added to the rear of the pier in 1979 lasted a brief period of time but foreshadowed a trend to come. The costly $400,000 investment was a precursor to the full-blown water parks that would emerge in the next decade, including the Raging Waters entities added by the Morey family at the back ends of Surfside Pier and Mariner's Landing. (Courtesy of the Wildwood Historical Society.)

For the 1980 season, Hunt's Pier debuted the Ghost Town Shoot Out interactive air rifle game next to Keystone Kops on the north side of the pier. The Wild West saloon theme fit right in with motifs of many of the pier's custom attractions, especially the nearby Ghost Town Junction and Golden Nugget. (Courtesy of the Wildwood Historical Society.)

The shooting gallery offered patrons a chance to test their skills by aiming at targets that, when hit, triggered various reactions. True success was defined by getting the piano player in the background to perform. Another favorite was the pump handle, which dispensed water into a trough while a mischievous-looking buzzard sat on top. (Courtesy of the Wildwood Historical Society.)

Five

THE TWILIGHT YEARS

In 1970, Bill Hunt passed away at the age of 98. Tributes poured in from his contemporaries within the entertainment and amusement industries, praising his accomplishments as a trailblazing entrepreneur. Locally, he was hailed as Wildwood's greatest businessman and a beloved community hero. Tragically, only five years later, Guy Hunt would die suddenly after ulcer surgery at age 66. The weight of the entire Hunt empire then fell on the shoulders of Bud Hunt, who would carry the torch for another decade.

The late 1970s and early 1980s proved to be a tumultuous time for businesses in the Wildwoods. As recession gripped the nation, the resort fell into decline. The Ramagosa family's long tenure on the Boardwalk ended when Sportland Pier was sold in the early 1980s. The Moreys moved quickly to fill the void, dramatically expanding Surfside Pier and acquiring Marine Pier East, which was soon to be renamed Mariner's Landing. Marine Pier West was sold to the Nickels family, who demolished the venerable Jack Rabbit/Screem Machine roller coaster and used the land for their own amusement center behind Castle Dracula.

In an age of economic uncertainty and unpredictable competition, Bud Hunt had some difficult decisions to make. He invested in the Ranger and Rampaging Rapids, theme park–like draws that again emphasized the attempts Hunt's Pier made to keep up with larger parks, such as nearby Six Flags Great Adventure in Jackson, New Jersey. The rapids ride, in particular, was a stark departure from the custom attractions for which the pier had been known.

Hunt's instincts were correct, as the ride proved to be a profitable addition. It would also be the final major attraction the Hunt family would install. By this point, Bud Hunt had already begun selling off other vestiges of his family's business empire, including its theater holdings and the Starlight Ballroom. After what was, by all accounts, a successful 1985 season, he completed the sale of Hunt's Pier to a group of local investors. Nearly 80 years after Bill Hunt first arrived in the Wildwoods, the end of a truly remarkable era had been reached.

Bud (left) and Guy Hunt (right) enjoy a moment with Wildwood mayor and Pier 6600 Motel owner Charles Masciarella (middle) at Ed Zaberer's Anglesea Inn. After the passing of Bill Hunt, the brothers inherited and split full control of the pier, movie theaters, and the Starlight Ballroom. When Guy died unexpectedly in 1975, shock waves were felt throughout the community. Bud, though deeply saddened by the loss of his younger sibling and business partner, continued on. He would remain in control of the family's various holdings for a number of years, but for the first time, the long-term future of the amusement park was in question. In the seasons that followed, Bud would put his own unique stamp on Hunt's Pier, adding several attractions that simply could not have been imagined when the park made its debut in the late 1950s. (Courtesy of the Robert J. Sully collection.)

By the mid-1970s, the pier had long since established itself as one of the finest amusement parks in the country. It wasn't the largest, nor by this point was it considered among the most spectacular, but it provided a safe, fun, unique environment for all members of the family. The crowds that appeared on the pier year after year were proof that the formula still worked. The Wildwoods and Hunt's Pier remained synonymous, though unbeknownst to most, its remarkable tenure of custom-showcasing fun was beginning to wind down. (Both courtesy of the Wildwood Historical Society.)

To the north, the Surfside Pier and Sportland Pier amusement centers continued to provide viable competition. Surfside, in particular, was growing by leaps and bounds as the Morey family built off of the success of their 1969 investment, the Wipeout! Slide (visible above, center). Subsequent additions of note included the iconic Kong ride and the Haunted House. Back at the "Oceanic Wonderland," old favorites shared space with new rides brought in on a regular basis to keep things fresh. Over the course of time, a small kiddie coaster and a double-decked carousel appeared as the park headed into the twilight of its glory days as the crème de la crème of the Boardwalk's entertainment scene. (Courtesy of Jackie and Jim Slaviero.)

Typical of any amusement park, Hunt's Pier was in a constant state of change. The roster of secondary rides was altered on a yearly basis, and new promotions were implemented before naturally running their course. Longtime Hunt's publicity man Merle Paul continued to play an active role in documenting the pier, photographing rides and attractions for use in various advertising campaigns. (Courtesy of the Wildwood Historical Society.)

The uniqueness of Hunt's Pier was reflected and at times defined by its colorful roster of employees. Louis "French Louie" Vendittelli, seen among the props of Jungleland, was well known as the longtime operator of the Golden Nugget. Behind the scenes, he was also the pier's head mechanic. (Photograph by Merle Paul; courtesy of Ralph Grassi, Funchase.com.)

Assistant pier manager Bill Blackburn was another skilled mechanic and one of the Hunts' in-house artists. The pier's operation was a well-oiled machine in large part due to its talented, versatile staff. Regardless of the project at hand, there were always multiple capable hands on deck to see it through. (Courtesy of the Wildwood Historical Society.)

The Hunt's Pier Photo Shack was added in the late-1970s near the Flyer at the entrance to the pier. There, guests could pose for photographs with some of the park's recently conceived mascots, including the Golden Nugget bear sheriff and the Skua's ship rat. (Courtesy of the Wildwood Historical Society.)

With space on the pier always in short supply, even larger rides and attractions were not immune to occasional relocation. The Whacky Shack, Keystone Kops, and the Skua were all eventually shifted around and moved to other locations on the pier. Due to the Skua's size, the structure was carefully placed over soap flakes and pulled by truck to the north side of the pier. Though the ship did not sway as dramatically as it did in its first few years of operation, the ride remained a major attraction in its new location and would continue to do good business for the next decade. (Both courtesy of the Wildwood Historical Society.)

Along with its relocation, it was determined that a new entrance for the Skua was needed. This terrifying pirate face structure was built by Jim Melonic in 1983, and it added a macabre touch to the ride's exterior presentation. That same season, the ship debuted a new gray and white color scheme. (Courtesy of the Wildwood Historical Society.)

The original skull-shaped cove remained in use as the new exit portal. A feature since the ride's inception, the green flood lights inside the eye sockets of the motif completed its menacing look. This was a particularly striking feature when viewed from a distance and, of course, at night when Skua's backdrop was the ominous black void of the ocean. (Courtesy of the Wildwood Historical Society.)

Of the Skua's many props, visual gags, and fun house–style surprises, no aspect of the ride is more fondly remembered than the famous tilted room. Patrons used guide rails to navigate the gallery, which featured a slanted floor designed to mimic the disorientation one would experience below deck on a sea-bound ship. (Photograph by David Nelson.)

Hunt's Pier ownership and management took particular pride in the park's reputation as a place for families. Here, three generations of the Murray/Slaviero clan from Taylor, Michigan, take aim at the interactive targets of the Ghost Town Shoot Out. Just about all attractions on the pier could be enjoyed by everyone in some way. (Courtesy of Jackie and Jim Slaviero.)

When the Nichols family, owners of Midway Pier, decided to raze the 65-year-old Screem Machine (formerly the Jack Rabbit) in 1984, the Flyer became the oldest roller coaster in operation along the Jersey Shore. The Hunts' inaugural flagship attraction was a cherished institution after almost 30 years of operation. It was not uncommon to hear of letters written to the owners detailing stories from those who rode the coaster as kids, only to return years later to share the thrill of the over-the-ocean adventure with their children and grandchildren. It is fondly remembered by countless individuals who claim it as their first roller coaster experience. (Both photographs by Richard W. Munch.)

Hunt's Pier continued to keep older rides and attractions fresh by periodically making changes. The Keystone Kops, which quickly became a favorite of children and adults alike, was updated with an appealing brick facade. Previously, the structure's exterior had sported 1960s-style psychedelic and "wildflower" designs. (Courtesy of the Wildwood Historical Society.)

The completed work gave the ride a new wooden railing to better accommodate lines. The bulb-studded lettered signage was also repositioned. Another new feature was large windows placed at either end of the ride. This allowed curious onlookers to get a sneak peek, including young children who were unsettled about what they might experience inside. (Courtesy of the Wildwood Historical Society.)

Hunt's Pier continued to import flat rides from Europe, and one of the flashier additions was the Musik Express. The combination of an impressive lighting package and loud music made for a successful update of the Caterpillar rides from the earlier part of the century. (Courtesy of the Wildwood Historical Society.)

The Spider was a flat ride that featured free-moving tubs that spun as the arms moved up and down while the entire platform rotated. The attraction, which sat near the Skua at the rear of the pier, was supplied by the Eyerly Aircraft Corporation and was an updated version of the company's popular Octopus ride. (Courtesy of the Wildwood Historical Society.)

94

No amusement park was complete without bumper cars, and the Mini Skooters occupied that place in Hunt's Pier's ever-expanding ride arsenal. This version, supplied by Italian ride manufacturer Bertazzon, was designed specifically for children. The ride was positioned on the south side of the pier opposite the Whacky Shack. (Courtesy of the Wildwood Historical Society.)

The Red Baron effectively replaced the aging Satellite Jets ride, although like the Mini Skooter, it was designed for the smaller members of the family. Children boarded alternating red and white World War I–era fighter planes equipped with flight sticks that allowed them to control the height of the aircraft as it rotated around the center boom. (Courtesy of the Wildwood Historical Society.)

For the 1982 season, Bud Hunt spent a whopping (at the time) $600,000 on a Ranger ride from HUSS Park Attractions of Bremen, Germany. The acquisition of such a thrill ride was a noted departure from the Hunts' tradition of adding more intimate custom attractions. (Courtesy of the Wildwood Historical Society.)

The Ranger's only passenger vehicle was brought to the pier in one piece, lifted by crane from the back of a flatbed truck on the beach during the winter of 1981–1982. An investment of $53,000 was needed to secure a concrete pad that could support the combined 40-ton weight of the ride. (Courtesy of the Wildwood Historical Society.)

Once installed, the Ranger added a completely new dimension to Hunt's Pier. This was particularly the case at night, when the ride's impressive lighting package turned it into a visual tour de force. The ride itself certainly wasn't for the faint of heart or the weak of stomach. The massive attraction tossed riders upside down as the huge boom rotated into the air. Not unlike the headliners of years past, the Ranger was well patronized and projected an undeniable mystique. One drawback was that this was strictly an adult ride, the only attraction on the pier that children were unable to enjoy. The Ranger certainly proved to be a worthwhile investment, at least in the short term. It was positioned toward the back of the south side of the pier, behind the Golden Nugget; there it would not visibly dominate the pier's other much smaller attractions. (Courtesy of the Wildwood Historical Society.)

By the early 1980s, the Ocean Center name had been dropped from Skyline Golf, which was now linked more directly to the pier. The instantly recognizable pylon, decorated with large, colorful neon signage, was perhaps the most prominent advertisement on the Boardwalk of its time. Here, it stands out on the approach to Twenty-sixth Avenue looking south. (Courtesy of Jackie and Jim Slaviero.)

Sourier Grotte, loosely translated as "Dinosaur Cave" or "Dark Grotto," was a dark ride imported from Germany that featured elaborate artwork highlighted by a giant skeletal dinosaur design and demonic characters atop the flashy facade. The relatively pedestrian interior of the two-story ride was not nearly as memorable as the exterior. (Courtesy of the Wildwood Historical Society.)

HUNT'S PIER   "AN OCEANIC WONDERLAND" - - -

Your FUN might start careening down the water chute on the LOG FLUME RIDE . . . Ride your own mine car and drop into unexplored mine shafts on the GOLDEN NUGGET MINE RIDE . . . Roam pirate caves and then board the GHOST PIRATE SHIP, "Skua" for new thrills . . . Join the jungle guide in JUNGLELAND aboard the "Congo Kitty" for a jungle waterway ride amongst animals and flowers . . . If you're seeking "super-duper ultimate thrills" – it's on the RANGER . . . The whole family can go for a ride aboard the IRON HORSE GHOST TOWN railway for real railroadin' fun . . . Zoom on the FLYER rollercoaster . . . Kooky fun in the WHACKY SHACK . . . Bouncing fun on the TIP TOP . . . Zany SPIDER thrills . . . Everybody enjoys the KEYSTONE KOP antique cars, the TILT-A-WHIRL, the SCRAMBLER, the RED BARON airplanes and the MINI bumper cars . . . Small Fry FUN can be found on the water BOAT ride, the MINI-JETS, the MINI-ENTER-PRISE and the HOT RODS! Extra fun . . . Miniature golfing on HUNT'S PIER SKYLINE GOLF . . . a garden penthouse overlooking the boardwalk and beach . . . Challenging excitement with the electronic guns at the GHOST TOWN SHOOT OUT . . . Have a HAPPY DAY on HUNT'S PIER.

Pub. by Leader Printers, 5914 New Jersey Ave, Wildwood Crest, NJ 08260

dp

Since its inaugural season, Hunt's Pier was touted as having something for every member of the family. As the pier expanded into one of the country's premier seaside amusement parks over the years, ownership never lost sight of the importance of variety. Yet, unlike most amusement parks that put their marketing efforts behind new additions, the Hunts also understood the value of longtime favorites and made sure to sell them to new patrons as well as repeat visitors. Promotional literature from the era made mention of everything from the pier's super-custom rides like the Flyer and Whacky Shack to flat-ride favorites such as the Tip Top and Spider and even Skyline Golf. Hunt's Pier changed with the times, but the core of the facility was always expanded upon instead of replaced. This c. 1984 image depicts the pier in its untouched glory. (Hunt's Pier promotional material, Dexter Press.)

Bill Blackburn (left) and Vince Kostek confer with a carpenter at the future site of Rampaging Rapids, supplied by Intamin AG of Germany, during the winter of 1984–1985. Meanwhile, the spiraling incline of Surfside Pier's Jumbo Jet, a headline addition of the mid-1970s and an ever-present reminder of the Morey family's rise to prominence on the boardwalk, looms in the background. (Courtesy of the Wildwood Historical Society.)

Another example of the pier introducing a ride concept made popular in the nation's larger theme parks, the $1-million attraction was a downsized version of rapids rides that simulated the thrill of white-water rafting. The positioning of the ride across the back end of the pier signaled the end of the park's expansion onto the ever-growing Wildwood beach. (Courtesy of the Wildwood Historical Society.)

Once the sprawling new attraction was completed, crowds flocked to the far end of Hunt's Pier to investigate. After launching from the loading area, the rafts would travel around the rear perimeter of the park, off the pier at beach level. The ride featured several splash-worthy dips and turns as well as areas where higher concentrations of water flow sped things up. (Courtesy of the Wildwood Historical Society.)

Riders lined up to enter their circular rafts four at a time. The seats were configured to face outward and in opposite directions; this was different from typical rapids rides in which riders faced the center. The additions of the Ranger and Rampaging Rapids—just three years apart—added a modern, theme park–like atmosphere to the back end of the pier. (Courtesy of the Wildwood Historical Society.)

The turbulent waters foreshadowed an uncertain future for Hunt's Pier. Less than a year after Rampaging Rapids was installed, the seaside park was sold to a local group of investors. The popularity of the new attraction would bolster overall ticket sales for at least a few seasons and helped ease the transition to new ownership. (Courtesy of the Wildwood Historical Society.)

After Bud Hunt completed its sale for $2 million, 10 times the amount his father, Bill Hunt, had paid for Ocean Pier a half-century earlier, the fate of the famed pier rested with the Hunt's Pier Associates. The Hunt family's tenure of excellence on the Boardwalk had come to an end, but its legacy had long since been cemented. (Courtesy of the Wildwood Historical Society.)

Six

POST-HUNT ENDEAVORS

The sale of Hunt's Pier marked the beginning of the end for the Wildwoods' most beloved institution. In 1986, Hunt's Pier Associates, a group of local investors headed by David Kami, assumed control of the park. The initial changes they implemented seemed minor, but without warning came the blow that would alter the landscape of the Wildwoods' amusement scene forever.

Convinced many of the pier's original custom rides were outdated and no longer appealing to a new generation of park guests, Kami and his partners demolished the Flyer, Jungleland, and Skua following the conclusion of the 1988 season. Replacing the rides at the back of the revamped Hunt's Pier was a massive tangle of white steel dubbed the Kamikaze. No doubt a response to the Moreys' addition of the wildly popular Sea Serpent on Mariner's Landing five years earlier, the coaster failed to achieve widespread popularity and ticket sales were never able to overcome the initial investment. Just three years later, it was gone. Soon, the Hunt's Pier Associates would be gone as well.

Prior to the 1991 season, the pier was purchased by Conklin Shows, a Canadian-based carnival operator. The location operated as Conko's Party Pier over a four-year stretch during which business continued to decline and many attractions sat idle for long stretches. Hunt's Pier's last hurrah came courtesy of the Catanoso family who, in addition to having a longtime presence in the Wildwoods, were operators of the Steel Pier amusement center in Atlantic City. With the assistance of Fitraco, a Belgium leasing company for amusement parks, and a bank loan, four Catanoso brothers and two partners invested $10 million to renovate the former Hunt's Pier, transforming it into Dinosaur Beach Adventure Theme Park in 1996.

The Golden Nugget, Log Flume, and rapids ride were reworked to fit in with the new prehistoric theme. To those remaining rides, several notable attractions were added, including the elaborate Escape from Dinosaur Beach dark ride, a fossil dig for children, an 800-seat amphitheater, and two US firsts: a Master Blaster water coaster and a spinning take on the classic Wild Mouse.

The Hunt's Pier Associates viewed many of the pier's classic rides as antiquated and decided to invest in new, state-of-the-art amusements. In order to make room on the pier, a demolition crew was hired in February 1989 to remove some of the most beloved institutions, including—to the shock and dismay of many—the Flyer. After having thrilled crowds for 32 years, the iconic wood coaster was unceremoniously torn to shreds on a cold, otherwise quiet winter afternoon. Former operations manager Vince Kostek, who retired after Bud Hunt sold the pier in early 1986, lamented to the *Press of Atlantic City*, "I was sick all last night over [the demolition]. I helped build the roller coaster and laid the first concrete slab on the pier. Part of my heart just left me." (Photograph by Tom Kinnemand.)

The steel jaws of a crane from the Albrecht and Heun Company of Cape May Court House, New Jersey, made quick work of the Flyer's wood structure. In just a few short hours, the roller coaster that took weeks to complete by skilled construction crews and thrilled visitors for more than three decades was broken into small pieces and hauled off to the county dump in Woodbine. (Photograph by Tom Kinnemand.)

The Kamikaze was constructed for the 1989 season to replace several of the pier's longtime favorites. A state-of-the-art steel roller coaster, it stood more than 12 stories tall and featured five inversion elements along nearly 2,800 feet of track. It was supplied by the Dutch manufacturer Vekoma. (Courtesy of Bill and Seph Cherkasky, darkinthepark.com.)

Despite the removal of several rides and attractions, space on the pier was still in short supply. The Kamikaze was configured with a unique support structure that allowed it to be positioned over the existing Rampaging Rapids at the east end of the pier. The close proximity made for interesting visuals for guests on both rides. (Courtesy of Jackie and Jim Slaviero.)

A clever play on David Kami's last name, the Kamikaze was heavily marketed on billboards and in radio advertisements that aired throughout the region. The steel monster was designed to provide the kinds of thrills usually reserved for patrons at the country's top theme parks. (Courtesy of Jackie and Jim Slaviero.)

In stark contrast to the Flyer, the Kamikaze was a modern steel coaster that featured design elements popular at the time, including a twisting first drop and tightly packed inversions. Despite its promise, the coaster was considered an inferior attraction, thanks in part to a jarring ride experience that many found extremely uncomfortable. (Courtesy of Jackie and Jim Slaviero.)

The Whacky Shack dark ride was retained, despite the demolition of several neighboring attractions. However, a modified facade brought with it a new name—Hunt's Horror. Gone were the swaying letters the ride had become known for, but much of the interior remained untouched, leaving a traditional dark ride experience. (Courtesy of Bill and Seph Cherkasky, darkinthepark.com.)

The owners of the New Hunt's Pier quickly discovered patrons did not feel modern additions were a suitable substitute for the classic attractions demolished prior to the 1989 season. The massive Kamikaze was removed and subsequently sold following the 1991 season. Severely lacking rides and attractions to compete with the ever-growing Morey Organization, the once-thriving seaside park struggled to find an audience. (Photograph by Rob Ascough.)

The remaining rides and attractions from the pier's glory days, including the Golden Nugget, were left waiting for the occasional visitor to arrive as ownership of the park was transferred to Conklin Shows. By the end of the 1994 season, with the removal of two more classic custom rides—the Keystone Kops and Hunt's Horror—the pier once again faced an uncertain future. (Photograph by Rob Ascough.)

The Catanoso family came to the rescue. After operating limited rides under the Atlantic Pier banner in 1995, they set forth to dramatically redevelop the pier as Dinosaur Beach Adventure Theme Park. The park was officially run by Family Kingdom, Inc., composed of principals Anthony III ("Tony"), William, Charles, and Joseph Catanoso, Taft Johnson, and Edward J. Olwell. (Photograph by Steven Felder.)

Dinosaur Beach would take advantage of the few classic Hunt's Pier rides that were spared by the companies that owned the pier following the sale by Bud Hunt. The Golden Nugget was given a makeover that introduced dinosaurs and archeologists to the dark caverns long inhabited by ill-fated miners and was renamed the Golden Nugget Mine Escape. (Photograph by Steven Felder.)

One of Hunt's Pier's most popular attractions, the Golden Nugget remained a marquee draw on Dinosaur Beach, despite the protest of some longtime fans who balked at the altering of the ride's theme. In the end, the majority of patrons were simply glad to see the ride running regularly again. (Photograph by Rob Ascough.)

The Log Flume was another longtime Hunt's Pier institution given a mild makeover when a rock canyon that surrounded the final splashdown was added. It was subsequently renamed the Long Neck River Log Flume. Such simple, theme-appropriate renovations allowed the Catanosos to save and allocate funds for other projects. (Photograph by Steven Felder.)

110

The park's centerpiece attraction, which the Catanoso brothers would attempt to build around, was the elaborate Escape From Dinosaur Beach dark ride. A 10,000-square-foot, rectangular-shaped metal structure was built on the north side of the pier to house the ride, which was highlighted by an encounter with an animatronic *Tyrannosaurus rex*. (Courtesy of Sally Corporation.)

The ride was produced by Sally Corporation of Jacksonville, Florida, with design by R&R Creative Amusement Design of Anaheim, California. In addition to numerous life-sized robotic dinosaurs, special sound, light, and wind effects were utilized to create the sensation of an oncoming storm. (Courtesy of Sally Corporation.)

In the interest of continuity, the rampaging dinosaurs were said to have been discovered in an ancient gold mine, directly tying the ride's narrative to that of the revamped Golden Nugget. The prehistoric theme was incorporated into as many of the pier's attractions as possible. Visible at right is the pier's gift shop, located within the Escape From Dinosaur Beach structure. (Courtesy of Sally Corporation.)

Heavily influenced by *Jurassic Park*, the blockbuster sensation of three summers prior, the ride's story line setting was the Atlantic Research Institute. An educational tour of the compound quickly became an escape mission after visitors were briefed that previously captured dinosaurs had broken out of their holdings. (Courtesy of Sally Corporation.)

Pictured from left to right, Dinosaur Beach president Tony Catanoso, Sally Corporation chairman John Wood, and R&R Creative president Rick Bastrup gathered to oversee the completed ride prior to its grand opening. Wood designated it a fast-track project; design work began off-site the previous November, and installation was complete by Memorial Day. (Courtesy of Sally Corporation.)

Though operating on a limited budget, the Catanosos sought out industry-renowned firms to ensure that the ride's design quality held up to the standards of their vision. The rock work and trees were created by Sightline Studios of Gainesville, Florida. The vehicles and track were supplied by Majestic Manufacturing of New Waterford, Ohio. (Courtesy of Sally Corporation.)

Other new additions to the pier included a fossil dig for children that was located underneath the Long Neck River Log Flume, a handful of new flat rides, and a small steel roller coaster located directly behind the Golden Nugget Mine Escape. In the true spirit of Hunt's Pier, Dinosaur Beach was carefully designed to feature something that would appeal to all members of the family. (Photograph by Rob Ascough.)

As during the Hunt's Pier years, Dinosaur Beach's midway was a busy center of activity that featured access to all of the park's attractions. This included the short-lived Scout 1 virtual reality ride located outside of Escape from Dinosaur Beach. Also nearby was the Namco Arcave (arcade) and various themed concession stands that sold items such as Bronto burgers, jungle salad, and lava fries. (Photograph by Steven Felder.)

With the Kamikaze long gone, the space available above Rampaging Rapids—now called Raptor Rapids—was available for the installation of a new ride. The Thunder Lizard was a revolutionary concept at the time; even in the post–Hunt family era, the pier was the site of several groundbreaking attractions. (Photograph by Rob Ascough.)

The first-ever installation of a Master Blaster, the Thunder Lizard was advertised as a combination of a waterslide and a roller coaster. In addition to featuring downhill sections typical of a waterslide, powerful water jets were used to propel riders and their rafts forward over gentle hills. (Photograph by Rob Ascough.)

After a strong inaugural season, the Catanosos invested another $3 million for improvements in 1997. This included a $1.2 million spinning Crazy Mouse, the first of its kind in North America and only the fifth ever built. Supplied by Reverchon, the steel coaster took two weeks to construct and debuted on June 18. (Photograph by Steven Felder.)

Other new attractions included a $500,000 Orbiter by AmTech and Ricky's Rocket, a 195-foot bungee tower ride. Future plans initially called for more additions as well as the construction of a water park, but it wasn't to be. Just as quickly as it emerged, Dinosaur Beach went bankrupt and ceased operations after the 1998 season. (Dinosaur Beach Promotional Material, courtesy of Steven Felder.)

Seven

ENTER THE MOREYS

The three-year existence of Dinosaur Beach offered Hunt's Pier a brief respite, but it was clear by the latter part of the 1990s that this former epicenter of seaside fun and activity was living on borrowed time. In early 1999, the Boardwalk Development Group, consisting of Joe and Pat Croce, Mark Benevento, and Peter Luukko, acquired the pier from Family Kingdom, Inc., for $3.8 million.

To the immediate north, Morey's Surfside Pier, which began with the installment of a simple slide in 1969, had long since evolved into a full-fledged amusement park. With world-class rides like the Great Nor'easter inverted steel roller coaster, Zoom Phloom, and Condor, the pier catered to a new generation of thrill-seekers while featuring something for the entire family.

During the 1980s, the Moreys invested heavily in developing the former Marine Pier into Mariner's Landing, adding the Sea Serpent steel coaster and Giant Wheel. These moves were as symbolic as they were profitable, signaling the family's rise to the summit of the Wildwoods' amusement scene. Eventually, the Moreys would also acquire Fun Pier, the Boardwalk's southernmost amusement center. It would be transformed into Wild Wheels Pier, and in 1996, it became the site of the massive Great White, the first wooden coaster to be built on the island since the Flyer debuted nearly four decades earlier.

With three industry-renowned amusement piers and two popular water parks in operation, many wondered what the Moreys' next move would be. That question was answered, at least partially, when it was announced that they had leased Hunt's Pier from Boardwalk Development for the 1999 season. The seemingly inevitable sale was completed the following year at an undisclosed price.

The past and present legacies of the Boardwalk collided as a result, with a direct business lineage now connecting the Hunt and Morey families. Questions persisted about the Moreys' plans for the old pier, essentially a concrete shell of its former self. With only the Golden Nugget and Log Flume remaining, they were left to make some tough decisions.

Grand prix racers zoom through the former Hunt's Pier midway, in the shadow of the dormant Golden Nugget Mine Ride. In the years immediately following its acquisition by the Morey Organization, space on Hunt's Pier was leased to independently owned operations, such as go-karts and helicopter rides. (Photograph by Al Alven.)

The site of the Flyer roller coaster became home to the gigantic Skyscraper from Gravity Works of Ottawa, Canada. Riders on opposite ends of the 160-foot, windmill-like structure reach a speed of 70 miles per hour in less than one second, making it one of the Boardwalk's more extreme thrills. Originally a privately owned attraction, the Skyscraper was eventually purchased by the Moreys. (Courtesy of the Morey Organization.)

The building that formerly housed the Escape from Dinosaur Beach dark ride was left in place and now serves as the Morey Organization's Boardwalk-based support facility. During the winter months, it functions as a storage area for vehicles and other parts for many of the company's amusements. (Courtesy of the Morey Organization.)

The warehouse is also used to rehabilitate components of several rides. The rolling stock for the Great White—the Moreys' wooden roller coaster and the headline attraction at Adventure Pier—are rebuilt every offseason. Other structures at the rear of the pier include a new paint shop and a depot/storage center for the Boardwalk's famous Sightseer Tram Car. (Courtesy of the Morey Organization.)

With the Zoom Phloom in operation at Surfside Pier, the Moreys donated the old Hunt's Pier Log Flume to Arnold's Park in northwestern Iowa. The small, struggling park immediately benefitted from the installation of the classic ride, which remains one of its most popular attractions. (Courtesy of Arnold's Park.)

"Paul Bunyan," the iconic lumberjack who kept watch over the pier from his perch atop the Log Flume, remains local. He currently sits atop a storage structure at the old Hunt's Pier–Dinosaur Beach boneyard in Erma, New Jersey, just off of Route 9. His future remains unknown. (Photograph by Ralph Grassi, Funchase.com.)

A distant memory by the time the Moreys acquired the pier, the Kamikaze was dismantled after the 1991 season and sold to Six Flags Over Georgia in Austell. It re-debuted the following year as the Ninja and is currently one of 10 roller coasters in operation at the Atlanta-area theme park. (Courtesy of Six Flags Over Georgia.)

The Catanoso brothers moved their Crazy Mouse up the coast, relocating it to Steel Pier in Atlantic City after Dinosaur Beach closed in 1998. Though the spinning coaster operated in Wildwood for only two seasons, it is recalled as a unique attraction that made its own contribution to the history of Hunt's Pier. (Photograph by James Nocito, CanobieFan.com.)

The Moreys pondered ways to restore the Golden Nugget, either as an operating attraction or in some other form. Ultimately, it was decided the costs to rehabilitate the aging ride were prohibitive. After the decision was made to demolish the legendary attraction, a ceremony to honor the Nugget was held on January 30, 2009. Amid bitter-cold conditions and biting ocean winds, an estimated 1,500 people turned out for the event. The Nugget's structure was stripped of its steel track and hollowed, allowing a portion of the crowd to huddle inside. Below, among those recognized on this memorable afternoon were, from left to right, Adam Revesz, American Coaster Enthusiasts New Jersey regional representative; Rick Davis, Dark ride and Funhouse Enthusiasts (DAFE); Tom Rebbie, Philadelphia Toboggan Company; Kristen Steindl, granddaughter of Bud Hunt; and John Allen IV, son of Nugget designer John Allen III. At right are brothers Jack and Will Morey, the executive vice president and president/chief executive officer of the Morey Organization, respectively. (Both courtesy of the Morey Organization.)

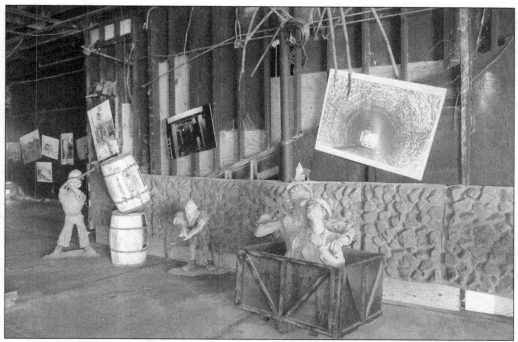

On display were some of the stunts that called the Golden Nugget home for almost five decades, including many original Bill Tracy classics. Some of the ride's props eventually found their way into other dark rides operated by the Morey Piers, such as Pirates of the Wildwoods and Dante's Dungeon. (Courtesy of the Morey Organization.)

The Nugget's ride's system was removed and sold to Knoebels Amusement Park & Resort in Elysburg, Pennsylvania. There, the track is being reconstructed as the Black Diamond for the 2011 season. The track layout and mine cars will remain the same, though the mine will be filled with all-new adventures. (Courtesy of Knoebels Amusement Park & Resort.)

Redevelopment of the front of Hunt's Pier began in 2005 with the completion of a two-story "Neo Doo Wop" structure that is home to the popular Sand Jamm Surf Shop. The building stands at the north end of the pier on the former site of the Flyer roller coaster's loading platform. (Photograph by Al Alven.)

In 2010, two more businesses would be added—Capt'n Jack's Island Grill and the Palace of Sweets. The latter houses a bulk candy shop as well as the Adventure Maze, which was designed by world-renowned maze designer Adrian Fisher. The structure itself was designed to resemble Ocean Pier's grand Funchase, a nod to the site's rich history. (Photograph by Al Alven.)

What can only be described as a fanatical devotion to the memories and icons of the "Oceanic Wonderland" is on display at the George F. Boyer Museum in downtown Wildwood. There, visitors can view a wide range of Hunt's Pier memorabilia, including authentic Keystone Kops characters and the Golden Nugget's skeleton cowboy (at right, minus his horse). Also on display are replica models of the Golden Nugget and Whacky Shack by Anthony Canzano and a replication of the Skua by David Nelson. The story of Hunt's Pier continues to be relived and explored from all angles. In early 2010, Scott Hand and Diane Pooler of Marksman Entertainment, Inc., began producing the multipart *Hunt's Legacy* documentary series. The films feature in-depth looks at the history of the amusement park as well as Hunt's Theatres and the Starlight Ballroom. (Both photographs by Al Alven.)

The future of Hunt's Pier rests in the capable hands of Will and Jack Morey (above, center). At the celebration honoring the Golden Nugget, the brothers unveiled plans for a second wooden roller coaster. Riders will begin their journey on Surfside Pier, then transverse a bridge-like structure that will carry them to Hunt's Pier. There, the train will travel over the former footprint of its ancestor, the Flyer, and many other super-custom classics. The massive attraction will not only be the first of its kind, it will physically link the legacies of the Hunt and Morey amusement empires in the Wildwoods. (Both courtesy of the Morey Organization.)

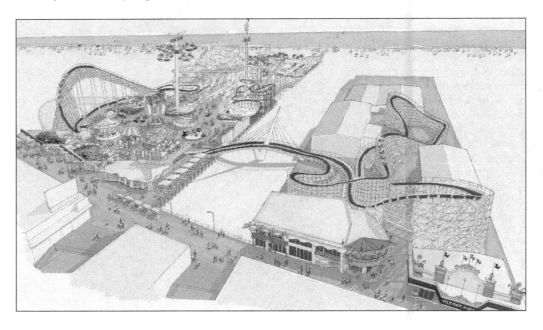

ABOUT THE SOCIETY

The Wildwood Historical Society was founded in 1963 as a tax-exempt, not-for-profit organization dedicated to the gathering, preservation, and presentation of the history of the Wildwoods, which includes Wildwood, Wildwood Crest, North Wildwood, and West Wildwood. The society was given new life by obtaining a building in 1990, leading to the creation of the George F. Boyer Historical Museum.

The George F. Boyer Historical Museum features vintage photographs, artifacts, and memorabilia depicting the various ages of the Wildwoods, from its merger with Holly Beach City to the present. There are special sections dedicated to the police and fire departments, beach patrol, boardwalk, history-making residents, and the scholastic and athletic achievements of the Wildwoods. The price of admission is a donation, and membership in the Wildwood Historical Society is open to any interested person or party.

A portion of the royalties from this book will benefit the Wildwood Historical Society as a way of thanking the exemplary staff members for their enthusiasm and tireless assistance in contributing to this project, which otherwise would not have been possible.

Visit us at
arcadiapublishing.com

CPSIA information can be obtained
at www.ICGtesting.com
Printed in the USA
BVHW010852250119
538677BV00007BA/14/P